DREAMING METAPHYSICAL

North of Eden Press
26 Loomis Street
Montpelier, VT 05602
802-229-4785
www.northofeden.com

Published 2010 by North of Eden Press
Printed in the United States of America
Copy edited by Patsy Fortney and Deb DeGraff
Cover and book design by Karla Van Vliet
Cover art, "Gravity," by Laura Ruth

The text of this book is set in Cochin.

ISBN-13: 978-0-9792415-4-3

Dedication

From Marc:
To Christa, the woman in my dreams,
who has always been Mary.

Other Books by Marc Bregman

The Deep Well Tapes
The Deep Well Tapes - The Secret of the Pomegranate
The Deep Well Tapes Audio Book

Hubris of the Heavens:
Archetypal Dreamwork and Rudhyarian Astrology

Dreaming Metaphysical

With Christa Lancaster

The Deep Well Tapes - Sex, Trauma and Conjunctio
which includes Christa Lancaster's book *Vessel*

Opening the Dream
The Theory and Practice of Archetypal Dreamwork-
A Video Introduction

Journeys of the Knight
Video Explorations of Archetypal Dreamwork
A DVD companion Book

Dreaming Metaphysical

By Marc Bregman

Edited by Susan Marie Scavo

North of Eden

North of Eden Press

from *Postcards from Cambodia*

This is too big for anger,
it's too big for blame.
We stumble through history so
humanly lame
So I bow down my head
Say a prayer for us all
That we don't fear the spirit
when it comes to call

by Bruce Cockburn

CONTENTS

Stage Two

Stage Three

Introduction to Dreaming Metaphysical

The process of teaching, writing and learning about the work has always been an intuitive process for me. I feel something come through me, then I speak it, allowing the intelligence to come through.

It is not that I am a puppet. The intelligence of what comes through me reflects my own sensitivity to the passion I feel inside, the passion that is somehow related to the Animus.

When this intelligence comes through me, I do not hear words exactly. It is more an energy of His will about something that needs to be expressed. I have some knowing of what needs to be expressed and then it just comes.

Anyone who advances in the work can develop their own intuitive calling – where they feel that energy inside, allowing it to come out. It can come out in art, in writing, in speaking (as it comes through me), in many, many ways.

I am simply someone who learned early in my life how His voice could come through me. How my passion, my frustration, my anger, my rage and my saying yes to my own process through fear and pain could come through and allow myself to be a living organism, an emotional expression.

Rather than someone who thinks.

Archetypal Dreamwork is not thought; it is felt. All

people who come into connection with their souls have the capacity to be in "felt work" rather than "thought work," no matter the venue in terms of expression.

I am proud to say that all of the students, teachers and leaders in North of Eden, not just me, are learning to do their "felt work." Christa Lancaster, my partner and my beloved, lives this felt work with me.

There are others who live this as well, each finding their own, unique way of expressing that "felt work": Susan Marie Scavo, Bill St.Cyr, Annie Wattles, Robin Chase, Dorothy Korshak, Karla Van Vliet, Laura Ruth, Bob Murray, to name a few.

Previous books I have written have each had a particular intention, some goal where we aspired to write about a certain level of knowledge. In the first Deep Well Tapes book, we worked on giving the over-arching, long view of this work. In The Secret of the Pomegranate, we explored the work through the lens of mythology; in Sex, Trauma and Conjunctio, we opened the issue of union with the Divine through the issues of sensuality and trauma, including Christa's spiritual memoir called Vessel. In Hubris of the Heavens, we showed how Rudhyarian Astrology can be a tool to elucidate not only specific dreams but also the larger, philosophical issues. In Journeys of the Knight, we set out to show the work through film and commentary.

But this book is different. This book is a place for me to speak what comes through in a new way. The essays in this book came from moments, came on their own, often during sessions when working with clients. Since writing the first four books, I have had my own deeper growth that continues to produce deeper insights. These are not focused on one thing, but are these moments.

I feel they may have meaning that may be of interest to you, to any who are interested in exploring dream metaphysics. The companion book to Journeys of the Knight DVD set is a cousin to this book, containing some of the included treatises that related to particular dreamers presented in the films. This book deviates from Journeys in that the essays stand alone. They are simply the raw expressions of those moments, those meandering moments of new material opening through me.

We hope to evolve this book through many editions in the future, if I continue to be blessed with more sparks of light.

The Child Self
Loss and Return

To find our true Child Selves, to claim the elixir of Divine Love, we must journey through our dreams to the core of our souls.

We begin our lives as the child self with a connection to the Divine. When a child is born, the ego is eclipsed by the child self, and the energy of id, libido, primalcy, love, The Boy, The Girl is fully formed. The ego filled with the child self has no self-awareness, no self-consciousness. The child self simply is: I am that I am.

By necessity, as we grow up, the child self recedes from the ego below the subconscious and into the unconscious. The gap between the ego and the child self is revealed in the discrepancies presented in dreams. Working with these discrepancies is the early work of the dreams. When we start to move into the feeling realm of the dreams, we start to tap into the child self.

Like ocean waves that wash up onto the shore and leave behind flecks of foam and parts of the ocean itself, the child self also leaves flecks or fragments of what was once a divine reality as it recedes into the unconscious. These spiritual fragments in the subconscious are not the wholeness of the child self. They are fragments of a gift, or the remembrance of something holy.

For example, a person may have a gift for music that is actually a fragment of something sacred that was once part of the wholeness of the child self. The ego takes this gift and builds an identity around it, but it is only a piece. We can tap some aspect of Divinity through prayer, meditation, art, and feelings in nature—because these things are left behind and can become a nucleus for good in us. But they are also things that the ego can use, which perpetuates our separation from the child self. The sacred fragment as identified with the ego has to die, or be let go of, for us to become the child self.

The child self is indomitable. The child self is a being we can know and feel. The wholeness of who He/She is, is greater than a particular action or fragment of a thing that we do. Psychology often helps a person acknowledge a fragment and incorporate that into the psyche. Sometimes those fragments are what we call gifts, but they are not the wholeness of the child self. Anything that feeds the ego but not the soul is narcissistic by definition.

Why go to the core of our being to become the child self? A child yearns for one thing. A child yearns for love. The moment of a newborn's cry is the same moment as our desire to be lifted up in the love. The need for love is the basis of the child's desire. The intention of the child self is to seek Divine Love. To find our true child Selves, to claim the elixir of Divine Love, we must journey through our dreams to the core of our souls.

In the subconscious there are memories of the past in this life and beyond this life. All the memories of our traumas as well as our spiritual achievements lie deep in the unconscious. That material then gets projected onto the outer world, sometimes in bizarre ways. For example, if you were raped in a past life, it may come up in this lifetime as freaking out when you look at a banana. You can go to therapy for five years and be able to eat bananas, but it does not mean you have solved the problem of the trauma. You have to go into the subconscious and the unconscious to reclaim the child self. Ironically, the way to go back is to feel all the good things and the bad things that have happened. Revisiting these feelings through the portal of the dreams is an extraordinary gift. Our choice as adults is—Will we go back to reclaim the child self? That is the work of Archetypal Dreamwork.

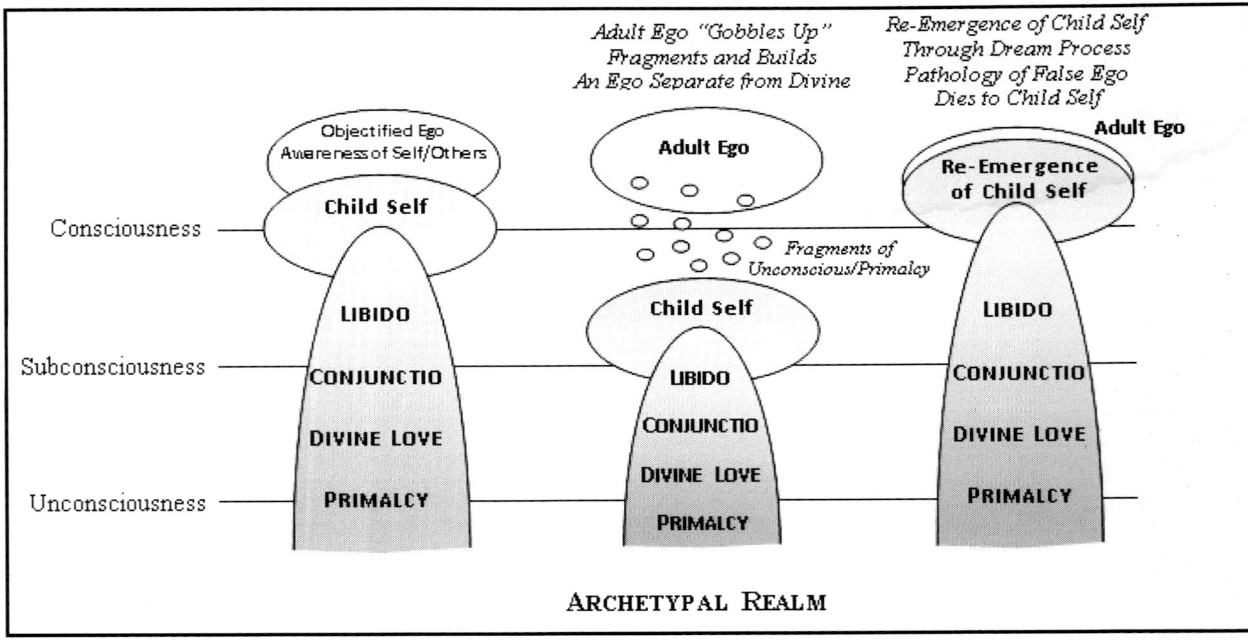
Adult Ego "Gobbles Up"
Fragments and Builds
An Ego Separate from Divine
Re-Emergence of Child Self
Through Dream Process
Pathology of False Ego
Dies to Child Self
Adult Ego
Objectified Ego
Awareness of Self/Others
Child Self
Adult Ego
Re-Emergence
of Child Self
Consciousness
Fragments of
Unconscious/Primalcy
Child Self
LIBIDO
LIBIDO
LIBIDO
Subconsciousness
CONJUNCTIO
CONJUNCTIO
CONJUNCTIO
DIVINE LOVE
DIVINE LOVE
DIVINE LOVE
Unconsciousness
PRIMALCY
PRIMALCY
PRIMALCY
ARCHETYPAL REALM

Stage One

Being Confessed

Every step we take in our work through our dreams, particularly in early stage work, is a series of observations that show us how we are not congruent with God or with our own soul. These observations are like confessions; we are constantly being revealed by the Divine through our dreams. If we accept the truth of the dream, it is a confession. But the difference is, we are not confessing; we are being confessed.

The Divine is showing us what it is we are confessing. We see not through some pathological reality but through the Divine truth of what is wrong, what is not congruent. What is being confessed is anything that is not congruent with our truth. It is not that anything is right or wrong, necessarily; it is about confessing how we are not in a relevant connection with ourselves.

This confessing is one step and then we have to really change. When the dream shows us what is wrong with us, what is out of alignment, it also helps us to realign. Part of that realignment, even though it occurs unconsciously in the core of us through the alchemical process, is applying those changes in the world. We can actually make different choices – refuse to listen to thoughts or emotions that we used to let control us that we now know are not true. We can do our homework of feeling into the real essence of our soul. These are choices that can be made hourly or every minute.

The War within the Psyche

Facing into our dreams through this work creates a war within the self. We are aware of the good/bad inside, but this is not about good or bad. Good/bad can often be a hydra of shame. The real war that gets unleashed through the dreamwork requires total, radical self-acceptance.

But most of us never really battle ourselves. We do not know ourselves well enough to see what the conflicts really are. When we work long enough with the dreams and with a dreamwork therapist to get to the point where the conflicts become obvious, then there can be a level of psychological work that is rarely seen in psychology. Most people project their conflicts into the world, and most traditional therapists try to manage this by giving advice and offering ways to minimize the pain.

But in reality, the nonprojected deeper pain and deeper conflict that is inside us is very real. That is the level this work can lead us into. Here, the dreamwork therapist has a whole new set of rules and understandings with which to work with others as they face into the war within themselves.

In this process, it is part of the therapist's work to create a vessel of acceptance, informing and challenging the dreamer but making sure that he/she knows there is always choice. Also, the therapist makes sure the dreamer knows it is okay to be wrong, to do it wrong, to not do it, to hate the work, to hate God, to feel resistant. All of this is simply pathology fighting back.

When the real war breaks open, the therapist is there to stand with the dreamer, helping him/her to know what is pathology and what is not, so that edge can be worked and opened even further. For the therapist, as one who can stand with another in this way, knows that this is part of the war.

THE HOLE IN EACH OF US

There is a hole in each one of us that can never be filled. That is because no matter what we obtain in the world, we still feel isolated and alone. We always aspire for more because there is always a vacuum. Even if we were to possess everything we wanted, we would still have that hole. Nothing would ever change.

Most of us never get that hole filled, so we die thinking our emptiness is because we never got the thing we wanted. We die not realizing that if we ever did get the thing we wanted, it would not have been enough either. It is always unrequited.

Unrequited love is a trick. It would never fill our thirst. Unrequited love tricks us by saying if we go for something we want and get it, then we will be fulfilled. That is a lie. If we got what we wanted, we would want something more or something else. That is what makes it unrequited. It can be anything, a relationship, money, a house on the beach, world peace or striving for inner peace. Unrequited love can be helping others or trying to make people feel better. It can be anything.

There is only one thing that can fill the emptiness of unrequited love: descent into the deep well.

We Have Already Been Devoured

There is the believe that we need to move toward feelings that are "good." This work, however, makes us feel uneasy for it makes us feel into the places where we need to go – into the disease – dis-ease, not into the ease.

The idea of dis-ease is the idea of disease – it is wrong, evil, bad, we will get sick, do not go there. But it is exactly in the place of dis-ease that the disease is because we failed to go through it.

And yet, this part of ourselves that wants to feel good challenges us. It is the Pleasure Principle of Sigmund Freud. We automatically go to what feels safe, pleasant, exciting, whatever we like, whatever makes us feel okay in the world even if it is completely dysfunctional. We choose it because it is better than the dis-ease we feel when we really go into our deeper feelings. To break this underlying NO and get to the uncomfortable feeling when our minds are telling us not to go there because it is bad. Not only do we need to go there, we need to live there..

This is where the alchemy takes place so that the uncomfortable feelings of the dis-ease change. One minute, it is dis-ease because it is new. Then it may move into deeper trauma, into pain and fear. Then it can move into joy and ecstatic experience. It can be anything because we are living in the miraculous.

When we put ourselves in a position of dis-ease, we are putting ourselves in a position where we are in God's hands. But because we have felt betrayed or violated in childhood we do not want to trust that process. We feel if we go to the unconscious world we are going to be devoured by demons. We have already been devoured by demons but our pathology tricks us to believe that we have not. Then we are terrified of the way out because we think the way out is really the source of our suffering. But in reality the source of our suffering is we do not leave.

This is why it is so difficult to take the work from the place where we finally see the choice and then actually choose to make the choice that brings us to Dying to Self. To enter the alternate reality of the Archetypal Realm.

But it is also a place of disempowerment because we do not get to run our own lives. Our lives become an extension of the life that we share with the Divine. Running our own life means we are isolated from Him. We can become sensitive to the fact that the dis-ease – the uncomfortability of being with the Divine in our passion – is actually what we really want. Once we reach this point, it is actually part of the dying to self.

But this is difficult because we have learned to survive on our own. The world keeps reminding us and teaching us that we have to continue to survive on our own if we want to survive. The world is not going to help us, but He is there to help. He is there even though we look around and we do not see Him. We do not see because nobody is in a place to receive it, not because He is not there to give it.

But we do not know that. We just look at the world and go, "Why would God let this happen? Why would God let that happen?" It reinforces the notion that there is no God, or if He is here, He is too far away to help, or He does not care like our father or mother did not care. We have all been hurt.

But, all the variations of how we step away do no really matter if we do the work our dreams would have us do. Eventually, we will feel the pain of wanting to be with Him. When we feel the need of wanting to be with Him, the work becomes a little easier. If we do not feel the pain or need, we are going to keep jumping away. We get tricked by the world.

But the pain anchors us if we are not afraid to feel it. Pain anchors us to what was lost and what we still desire in our deepest hurt. What we desire, ultimately, is Him. Sooner or later, when we do this work deeply enough, we will arrive at the place where we realize we do have this great love for Him. Because, somewhere, we remember.

The Split

In dreams, there is always a split between what the Archetype is bringing and our ability to understand and receive it. The split is there until it is gone. When we live that split, we are living in congruence with the world, not with the Divine. The Divine does not live in that split.

When that split is healed, however, when we die to self and that split is gone, we are no longer a card-carrying member of the human race. We are more connected with the Archetypes and our consciousness changes in a radical way – a way that most people will never understand. We lose our identity in the world. We are no longer a member of the human race in the way that people are members of the human race, for while the split in us is gone, the split is still there within everybody else.

Once we have found Divine love and have been healed of our wounds, however, we often will continue to project onto the happiness we see in the world. Even when we are beyond the place where the world has a hold on us.

What is it in us that we continue to hold on to the world or hold on to others – our families, our friends – in a way that is not about seeing how people suffer in a painful world but that becomes evocative of our own victimization or woundedness? When we feel hurt again about how people are separated from us in the world, then we are not accepting leaving the world.

To accept leaving the world is to accept that the pain we feel is not that we are victims of others but rather the pain of leaving the world is the pain of knowing it is no one's fault.

We have to accept that we no longer fit into this paradigm because we have the love that is sorely missing in the world. We have to take responsibility for the separation that increases with our family and friends as we grow. When we make it about them betraying us again, we are back to the beginning, as if to say, "I really want to belong to the world; why do you not accept me?" Rather than, "I am leaving a place that does not accept and know love. It is just a painful reality that I am leaving."

Until we are willing to stand in the split or the place where we look for love from the world – love that can only come from the Divine; until we see how when we use standing in the split to find some meaning in the world, even if it is by going into isolation or nihilism or if it is by going into existentialism or religion or hope, all of which can be pathology; until we can take full responsibility for our relationship with the Animus and accept it, then it is easy to believe that the world or somebody in it owes us something.

As soon as we step back into the split, we have our way. The attachment re-adheres. We are left with the projection – we can project our suffering and our unfinished work onto the world rather than onto Him.

Inverting Consciousness

There are two ways we reference ourselves – objectively and subjectively. For this work, the objective reference begins at the time we give up our soul selves – the polymorphous child, the intuitive/non-judging self – to become the part of the self that says, "I am."

From the "I am" place, we can reflect back on ourselves, our self-awareness. But if we use our self-awareness to judge ourselves, then we are truly lost. When we do this, it is like being on the wrong side of the mirror – we are not looking at ourselves at all. Instead, we are looking at a fabrication of ourselves that has nothing to do with who we are and what we really feel. It is impossible to take concepts of ourselves based on our blind spots and then do the work of acknowledging who we are or growing.

Subconscious understanding, on the other hand, comes from the soul. The soul that we do not feel or know looks out on us and realizes that our self-awareness is not in harmony with its awareness. The true self-awareness, the awareness of the soul, is lost to the objective self, which is busy fabricating itself.

There is this incredible split in everyone. We cannot heal ourselves when we are living in the objective self. When we ask, "Who am I and why am I here," the question begets the answer. We do not know the answer because we are not our true soul selves. If we were our soul selves, then we would know why we are here; we would know who we are.

If we cannot answer the question and feel the truth of it, we will never know who we are or why we are here. The very question actually says, "I do not know anything! What is my problem?" When we come into the work, we discover that we do not know the answer. In fact, the point is that we do not know.

When we realize that we do not know, it can be an opportunity for the dreams to step in, for the Animus to say, "I know who you are! Let me show you." The soul in us will stir and say, "I am the part that does know." With the help of the Animus or Anima, we can then reflect upon the self that we do not know – the soul self – because we are then looking for the answer from somewhere deep inside. From the place within, there is the Archetype saying, "I know who you are; I will find you; I will bring that true part of you up; I will help you to make that real."

Consciousness inverts. This is what we are doing, inverting reality. It is difficult to let go of ourselves because in the process, we are letting go of the world, letting go of everything we know.

When pathology fights back, it has only two choices: fight within or project the fight out into the world so that we are in conflict with the world. But we are not really in conflict with the world. When we react to the world in this way, we are really reacting to ourselves, reacting against ourselves.

This fight gets projected into the world so that the conflict we feel inside is suddenly living outside. In this place, self-hate may get reflected in choosing partners who do not like us, for example. Do we then get to work this out in the relationship? Do we change them or ourselves? We may think we are reconciling, but we are not. We may think we are getting better, but we are not.

When we try to get better, we are not really getting better – we are just adapting, compartmentalizing, accumulating knowledge, learning. The ego grows, but the ego is not the soul, so we grow in the wrong direction. We empower the wrong thing.

When we change to the subjective self, to the soul's point of view, everything can change. Everything.

Finding a Niche in the World

The problem with being the best looking or the nicest or the most fun or the one who has it all together or any way in which we find a place in the world is that then others around us expect us to be that certain way. This puts us in one of the biggest prisons of all. We may get the best jobs or have lots of friends and lovers, but we cannot be who we truly are.

Some people create a persona, like Hello Kitty or a Quacking Duck or Barbie, in order to find a niche on the bell curve. Maybe we all do this, but we have to grow out of the niche and realize that we are unique in ways that maybe we do not even understand and that have nothing to do with the world's acceptance or expectations.

We all have gifts that are on a soul level, but all pathology has to do is make us believe that we are not worthy. When we believe this, we are tricked into being a persona, which is really some aberration of personality that we create in order to make ourselves special.

Of course, this does not work – the reality is that our persona is a prison, for once we become the persona, we believe we have to be that person we have created.

In the meantime, we are really just scared. We can feel

like we do not belong, that we are not part of anything. We can try to keep pretending, but it is to the detriment of ourselves and of our relationship with Him.

Those of us who have found a way to thrive on finding a niche, on pretending, have a difficult time breaking the persona, which is really Dying to Self, because we have more to lose, more to give up.

Being Doted on or Doting on Children

When we have not been doted on, we may try to achieve satisfaction by being the doter rather than the dotee. As the doter, we do not have to worry about being the dotee because as long as we have love to give to our children, we can defer the issue of our own suffering. We love our children in the hopes that they will return the love, which they rarely do.

Even if they do, sooner or later, they leave us with an empty nest. In the meantime, however, we can defer our suffering for as long as we have our children. If we have many children, we may never have to face our suffering because we are always dealing with the children. And there is a great deal of satisfaction in this.

But the best parents are the ones who are doted on by the Divine in their everyday lives. They are not burned out, they do not overly stress with their children, they do not project their fear onto their children and make their children scared. This is a great gift to a child, to have parents who are connected with the Divine. But parents, especially mothers, have a huge blind spot around being parents. They believe they are the best, no matter how dysfunctional they might be.

The bonding process for the mother begins as soon as she takes the baby to her breast and looks at the perfection of the child. The child is, indeed, perfect, and that perfection is noteworthy. But a woman's bonding with a child is more than this for the mother is usually projecting her own child self onto the child. She does this because the child came from her. Most mothers do not do this with other children, just their own.

Of course, there are those women who love babies and can bond with any baby. But for the most part, there is no other cry like the cry of our own child. The most important bond is between mother and child. But the nature of this bond is basically narcissistic.

It is fundamental that mothers feel that their child can do no wrong, but this is narcissistic in nature for the mother is getting satisfaction for herself from the baby she produced. The mother does not get any satisfaction from God. The satisfaction comes from the baby's dependency upon her and for having "achieved" such a beatific child. The greater the bond, ironically, the greater the attachment, the greater the narcissism and the greater the reaction of the child. Both good and bad.

As a result, the mother will often ostracize the father from the child. She may have postpartum depression and feel she is left out in the extreme. The vagaries of women's reactions to their children are very personal but typically are predicated on the amount of love they have for themselves. The greater the love they have for themselves, the greater the love they have to give.

Of course, there are loving parents and some great mothers in the world, but people are very neurotic. This neurosis is passed down to children in the way the mother responds to the child. The perfection can sour very quickly. The mother may compete with the child or if there are multiple children, the child may get lost when the mother becomes over-burdened. There are many ways for the bond to be lost.

The bottom line is that to the extent that the mother is disconnected from the Divine, from her own soul, she will often act out in strange ways with her children to substitute for her own lack.

The greater the issues with the mother; the greater the problems with the child. The greater the abuse of the mother; the greater the likelihood that this is passed on through generations.

In dreams, when a woman who is a mother has a child, the most important thing to remember is that she is the child. The birth of the child in the dream requires her as the mother to die to the child, to become the child so that an archetypal parenting process can unfold. The more the woman dotes on the child in the dream, the more she maintains her position as mother, or, in other words, the more she maintains her position as goddess. For in the process of being a mother, she is a goddess, which is how it is presented in a matriarchy.

The celebration of a child being born in a dream is much better than the woman rejecting the child, because rejecting the child would be rejecting the soul self and can be more disabling than mothering the child. But, even when the mother celebrates the child, she still must become the child, she still must die to the child. The mother is the one who needs to be celebrated and doted on. The problem is that, usually, such a woman does not feel doted on at all. She may not even want to be doted on.

PROJECTING LOVE

If the love does not come from inside, if love is not felt as passion, as God's Divine spark that enables us to exist, we project that love onto an object or a person. When we do not have a connection to the inside, we seek the love outside. When we do this through projection or transference, we cross the line into narcissism.

The love that comes from the inside is free, powerful and does not require anything from anybody. We love because we feel the love. This is the prize. If the love is projected onto an object that is to be desired, then it becomes narcissistic. We want the thing for ourselves and in terms of our own agenda. Maybe we want to feel good, to avoid our shame, our pain, our insecurity. Maybe we want to make others responsible for all the things we are not facing because we cannot get the love.

In the end, we are bereft.

When someone loves us but only to meet his/her own needs, then there is an agenda attached to that love. It is not unconditional. This is projected love. An example is parents with an only child. They may want their child to do and be everything they could not do or be themselves. This is narcissistic love.

They love the child, but only in terms of their own needs.

There is a love that transcends need, narcissism, abuse. The love that comes from the inside allows us to love without that narcissistic need. This does not exclude relationship, need for others, marriage, and so on. It does mean, however, that there is a love that does not use us. There is a purer form of love that is embodied by the Archetypes, by the inner world or spirit. We recognize and know somewhere inside that this love does exist. We just cannot find it because we keep looking for it outside. True spiritual, enlightened souls have the love from the inside. These are the ones we look toward as teachers.

We are afraid of falling in love because love actually has a dark side. Once we are in love, we are chained to each other's pathology. It is like we have to take care of each other in a way that is dishonest. Falling in love can be tremendously bad unless both people have tremendous integrity and bring to the relationship their own sense of being loved by the Divine. From this place of being loved, we have something to offer to the other person. To the degree that we do not have the place of being loved, we have nothing to offer but a black hole of need and conflict.

The man may become possessive and not let his partner work or see her friends. In this scenario, he projects all of his insecurity as a male onto her and does not want her to do anything that would scare him. Women, too, project their anxiety and fears onto their partners. The result is that we enslave each other through what we call love. He says, "I love you," and beats her for going out with her friends. She says, "I love you," and beats him down because he watches too much football or he gets food in his teeth or he makes her look bad.

Even so, most of us talk a great deal about commitment to our partners. This is the Big Lie. Why should we commit to something that does not even exist? Why should we commit to being controlled by another person because the other person has no self-worth? Both men and women are like this – we want our partners to give us self-worth, but it can never happen.

Feeling Good is Not the Answer

Most forms of feeling good are really only addictions to something external. When we feel good in this way, the feeling good is on top of our deeper feelings and our separation from our souls. Feeling good can be spiritual – prayer life or meditation – or it can be things like cars, food, mountain climbing, Greenpeace, right wing, left wing, up, down. Anything.

Whatever we do, even if it is good and it makes us feel good, can be an addiction to feeling good by virtue of something external. It may even massage the soul, but the soul does not want to be massaged. This is like Chinese torture to the soul. The soul wants to be free, to manifest in the world.

Feeling good is not the answer. The idea of choosing spiritual feelings over suffering is not the answer. The answer is to be liberated from the suffering of the old self. The suffering must be plunged to its depth, to its core, which is how the soul is liberated. This is the alchemical process, the most mysterious of all spiritual endeavors.

There is a distinction between feeling good and the feeling good that comes from the liberation of Dying to Self. From the place of freedom of the soul, we feel exhilarated but it does not mean we do not feel pain. The soul always feels pain;

pain is love.

When the soul is free, there may be even more anxieties. These may reflect some deeper work to be done or they may be the nature of new growth. These anxieties and fears are tolerable, however, because they do not arise from the separation from our selves.

Whereas, if we artificially, aesthetically, spiritually hold on to spiritual feelings; if we cover our deeper pain; if we do not go through the process of true healing, then we cannot flow from feelings of exhilaration to pain to joy to love to pain to grief to.... This is the way the soul really operates when it is free. When the soul does not hide a deeper issue, it just feels through the feelings.

But when we are hiding deeper traumas or separations from the self, then we cannot flow back and forth very easily. Each step into feelings is experienced like a drop into the deep well – fathoms deep.

But at the bottom, there is no more drop. At the bottom of the deep well is true water. The bottom of the deep well is where Persephone journeyed. It is the essence in all pain and love and pathos without the tragic consequences of our separation from the Divine self or from God.

Feelings that are reflective of connection are very different from feelings reflective of disconnection, or that reflect fragmentation of the psyche. To understand this is to explore the bottom of the well.

When we are at the bottom, we can see the difference between these feeling and the feelings we went through when there was more drama and emotional separation. Going through feelings that reflect deeper feelings is more difficult than just being in our core self.

The Centrifugal Force of Pathology

The centrifugal force that prevents us from being with the Animus is merely the winds, the maelstrom of the pathology. It is spinning. When we are going around and around, it is reflected as certain patterns or predictable behaviors that we do not even recognize as a pathogen.

We think we have control over the spinning, but we do not. So when we try to drop down through that spinning energy to the core of our feelings, there is a conflict that wants to pull us out of that. But the Animus stands right in the center of that spinning.

He is in a timeless place that says *Come through, Come here, Come to where I am.* It means to become who we are. This means dropping down through trauma, dropping through pain, dropping through fear and moving through all the feelings that we have denied. That denial is what throws us into the spinning. To come through the spinning, we must go through all of these feelings to arrive at a place of ground zero.

The Animus will work through what needs to be healed, loved, supported or moved through by the process of alchemical change. It is all part of allowing Him to work with us. But as long as we are spinning, He cannot reach us.

Our reactions to the Animus, or what we think of as resistance to Him, are really our ways of resisting facing our own real feelings. If we do not want to deal with our real feelings, then we really do not want to deal with Him.

When we cannot stay with ourselves, we cannot stay with Him. If we can be in our pain and our feelings, then it is easier to be with Him because we are not blocking ourselves. He stands where the soul is and where our feelings are. When we can acknowledge and stand with our feelings, then He can stand with us, even if our feelings are difficult or discordant.

How Shame Steals the Choice

When we have shame, the idea of surrender feels terrible. We feel if we let go of our pride, we will flip into our most unworthy self. If that is the case, we cannot really give ourselves over to the Animus because He will find out what we already know, that we are unworthy. In this way, pathology holds us hostage with shame. We then put layers of pride on top of it, trying to be in control.

A person who lives a simple life can be as arrogant as a person with wealth who chooses to show off that wealth. There are people who have a lot of money with the intention of showing off, without enjoying the abundance at all. Whether we flaunt our poverty or our wealth, it is still showing off. Why do we show off? Because we feel terrible about ourselves.

Shame can be an excuse or what causes the excuse – it controls us either way, even if we are not looking for an excuse. When this shame is gone, maybe we will feel passion or dispassion or fear or excitement. Who knows what feeling will come up. But the moment we do not have shame as an excuse, we have a chance to make a choice.

Shame does not give us that opportunity. Shame drives us into pride and reaction and trying to manage ourselves. When we do not have that external projection of shame into the world anymore, where do we go?

In that moment when shame is no longer an issue, we have the opportunity to find ourselves and choose to take the journey. The journey is not about something that has any attachment to the world at all. It is between us and God. Finally. When we feel pain and regret that we did not go on the journey, it is proof that we are ready to go. The pain is our passion. The pain says, "It is time; I want to go."

How Pride Steals Our Hearts

The soul always needs the Divine, like a child in a dream who always needs the Divine. Always. The difference between us and the child is our attachment to the gyroscopy – our pride and shame. It confuses us or distracts us in a way that we forget we need Him.

Many of us who face death turn to God in that moment, even the most devout atheists. But then when things go right again, we go back to our pride. The pride, the pathology, will not go into death with us. As soon as we get close to death or crisis it disappears. Pathology does not deal with death – physical death or psychological death.

Pain makes us want the Divine. Pride's purpose is to have us not feel. It lulls us into feeling good, or distracts us by saying that other things will make us feel good – which they will not – if only we will forget our pain, our need and our loss.

And we do forget. We are so willing, because pain hurts and we do not like to hurt. But pain allows us to be vessels for love. Without the desire, without the pain, there is no desire for God. Pride steals that from us.

Shame is different. Shame does not seduce us, but gives us the power to control. It is a distraction. If we feel ashamed, then we do something to be better. If we do not like our clothes, we go get some better clothes. If we do not like the way we look, we lose weight. Whatever it is, shame motivates us to do better.

Shame and pride work together, but pride is more subtle. Pride tricks us into being content with things that do not offer contentment. It makes us think we are happy when we are not. It makes us think we are satisfied when we are not. Shame takes away our right to have pain. But pride does something worse; it gives us a feeling of fullness like bad carbs or sugar. It steals our hearts from us. And we do not even know it. With shame, we at least know something is wrong.

Of course, the gyroscopy of pride always works against this opposite pole. The opposite of pride is the belief that we are unworthy or inadequate or guilty or not special. All that is to say, unworthy of God's love – assuming we even believe there is such a thing.

On the other side, pathology says, "You know what? I'll give you this instead. I'll give you this sense of well-being, so that you do not have to feel that you are so bad, so unworthy, so dark. So that you do not have to be vulnerable and be cut down in your prime. You can be something anyway, even though this world has it in for you. Or even though God has it in for you, I, your pride (which is the ultimate demon), I will empower you. I will give you the strength of five men!"

But before we can believe this lie of pathology, we must believe the first lie that we are nothing. Once we believe we are nothing, it is easier to believe the second lie. The second lie is either that we are going to fall into a big puddle and drown or that we are going to stand up and be whatever we want anyway. This is a form of anger. It is like saying, "I AM going to make myself into something anyway, even though it will destroy me. I am going to stand up and say *Screw you* to everyone."

We do not have to do everything ourselves, like a scared little boy swinging his fist at everything that comes close to him, convinced that everyone is going to hurt him.

That is typical of a fatherless son. He is just hurt, angry, feeling unsupported and striking out at anyone who seems, in any way, shape or form, to be any kind of threat. Which basically means anybody more powerful than him.

The lie of the pride is, if something greater than us has power, then we are nothing. Pride wants us to believe this, because then we will never trust God, never trust the Divine.

Rewounding Through Projection

Each time we want something from someone else or from the world, we rewound ourselves. Our wanting from others is a projection of a desire that can only be met by the Divine. Rewounding ourselves through a projection only reinforces our belief that the problem is outside, that it is with someone else, that we are innocent and people are not there for us.

In fact, if someone were there for us, if God were there for us, we would not feel it anyway because we would be too busy managing. Always the perpetual victim who feels sorry for ourselves.

On some level, we are innocent, but we do not realize that we can no longer be fulfilled. It is the Big Lie of the mother that it is the father's fault or it is the child's fault or the child feels it is the parent's fault.

We have to go to the wider circle of the Divine reality where we know we were all born of that. We have to find that thread which is rampant in our dreams. The Archetypes are everywhere in our psyches – not to give us messages, but to love us again.

We have to be willing to go back through the wound

and the fears and the insecurities and even go back through things that may have happened in past lives – not just in this life. It is a torrent of history that makes us what we are; hurts and disappointments make up our history.

We must learn to feel this child and all the hurts underneath rather than blaming or expecting that somehow other people are going to do for us what they cannot even do for themselves. No one can help anyone really.

For those of us who caretake, this is a revelation for we try to take care of everyone else in the way that we wanted them to take care of us; "I'm not getting the love I need, so I will love others in the way that I need and maybe I will get the love I need from them." But it does not happen and the love we are so proud of giving others is not real because it is completely conditional – we expect something back.

Love does not want anything back.

Even if the other person gives us what we want, we are still wounded. We have got to take that wound and introject it, bring it back through a dream where we can face into it inside. It is very tricky to do because once we put our wound outside of us, everything in us wants it to resolve in the world.

When we feel the pain without the projection, it is incredibly raw. This is why we would rather project, because it is not as painful. It is also why we blame others. We can get angry; we can justify. But if we turn it back to our inner work, bring the projection back to ourselves, it melts the reaction away.

Caretaking

The difference between being a caring person and being a caretaker is that the caretaker avoids feelings by caretaking another person. When we are caretakers, we do not want the other person to feel feelings that we do not want to feel ourselves – usually pain or fear or shame.

When we are caretakers, we are very manipulative and very controlling. We are always in charge, always in control, always managing. As caretakers, we are also often compulsive; when we are done taking care of others, we clean the house, recycle, do something else. A caretaker's work is never done.

When we are caring and loving, we do not avoid our own feelings and we allow others to go through what they need to go through. We do not have to manage or control the situation. There may be times when we take care of another person, but we are not compulsive and we can respond to what is needed based on the situation, which is often unpredictable.

Caretakers end up locked into being a certain way or managing in ways that create a regimentality, a sense of duty. It is all so that we do not feel. The tricky thing about caretaking is that we believe we are feeling. If we are not angry, numb or resentful, then we feel that we have done a good job, and we have pride about having done something for someone else.

When we say that we have "felt another's pain," if we are empathetic, we may not have felt the other's pain, only concern for the pain. The question in this situation, however, is: Are we really feeling another's pain, or are we feeling our own pain?

When the other person is in pain and it is a person who betrayed or abused us, for example our mother, then maybe we feel the pain of how we have been betrayed and instead of really feeling that, we "feel into her pain." The pain then is the pain that the person who abused us gave to us. Caretaking someone who abused or even is currently abusing us is a terrible thing for the psyche.

Caretaking is not just about being compulsive around repressing our own feelings. We often caretake people in order to be good enough to be loved. In the case of a child with a mother who is not present in some way, the child caretakes the mother so that the mother will love the child.

But even if we are "perfect," we do not get the love because we are always trying to be "better," which means being different than who we are. We are never satisfied.

INTENTIONALITY

When we look for results, we have intentionality. For example, when we do or say something in order to have another person like us, then this is looking for a result.

This is different from saying or doing something when we are in our soul self, for when our soul wants to do or say something, this comes from being in the passion of the energy of the soul self. There is no intention beyond doing or saying. We may also not speak or not do something because it does not feel right, in response to our connection with the Animus. This is also different from having our own intentionality, for it is being without intention, which is really being in His intention.

Before we can surrender to His intentions in this way, it is important to know our own intentions. If we do not know our intentions, then we have unconscious intentions and are not able to be in His intentions. We will be led down the wrong road.

Knowing our intentions is part of knowing our own pathology. When we do go deep enough, we will not care about these intentions because the soul self, the child self, has no intentions. The child's sense of identity is just to be expressive, to be with the love, to be with the connection to the Divine, to be with its own energy.

The child/soul self does not have a bicameral experience where it objectifies reality and lives in the world of cause and effect. The child only knows what it feels. We as adults do not know what we feel; what we do know is what we want and what we would like to have, but these are usually all in the outer world. The child knows what it feels and does not care about the outer world. The child already has what it has and what it needs. The child is already autonomous. It does not need anything in the world and so does not need a goal to achieve something. The child is achieved by having itself.

When we understand our intentions, we can give them to Him and allow our only intention to become wanting Him. Our dreams show us how to be in that place of desire with Him. Then, all other issues fall away.

This can be difficult to allow because it kills the very fabric of what we believe about who we are. Often, we become the agents of intentionality, which is our personality, our sense of identity. That which achieves the goal of the intention.

When all of our intentionality dies away and all we are is the child, walking with the Divine in a clear and innocent way, then our relationships in the world become equally clear and innocent. There is nothing to want. When we want nothing from the world, then we can listen. We are just being obedient, rejoicing that we have finally done what He wanted, which is what we want. He is there to support us – this is where the love is.

Sometimes our intention is to get love. As long as we do not get the love, but instead get conditional love in the world in a way we can understand, we can continue to have intention. Even when we are getting love in the world that is not conditional. The love that we get is not really love for we are selling ourselves. When we get love in this way, it feels as if people are loving us for no good reason.

When we have a dream to contradict this way of living, we may react. What if we have a dream where we are affirmed and loved by the Divine for no real "reason"? We have done nothing, have not performed cartwheels or compromised ourselves sexually or been a caretaker in order to get the love. We have not said, "Yes, ma'am" or "No, sir." If we are not the child self being loved in this dream, we will not understand. If we have jumped far away from our child self, our soul self, receiving the love without our own intentionality may cause us to sabotage the love.

We sabotage the very thing and the very people who care for us. Not everyone does this, of course, but if we are not ready for the love, we are not ready to die to the love. Even if we do everything it takes to allow the love but are not ready for it, the love burns right through us and we may want to get it out.

Love kills because most intentionality comes from the lack of love. When our egos are set up to get something and then we receive it, leaving us without our intentionality, we question who we are. We have no reason to live the way we have been living. It is difficult to accept being the beloved, receiving the love, especially if we are not yet in our soul self to receive the love.

In truth, we are afraid of the love. It is a pivotal reality of this work.

The deeper we go with the Animus, the more love we feel and receive, the deeper we go into what is left of our trauma – and the deeper we go into our fear. This is one reason why we are afraid. When we get the love, we do not immediately feel healed. We are, ultimately, but we often have to go into deeper regions before feeling healed.

But we can go to those deeper regions because the love is there. We cannot really enter into our core feelings without an awareness of Him, because we would probably go crazy.

When we feel alone in the world as children, we feel

there is no one to trust. The idea of monsters under the bed is simply a projection – we know the world is unsafe or that adults, or even our parents are unsafe. Maybe we realize that our parents are not gods and this must not be heaven anymore. Maybe we realize this is not where we came from – where we come from is probably a better place.

All of this gets projected out. This is the core trauma for many people who have not been traumatized in a physical or sexual way as children. We know we are not with God and we feel terror.

Without having intimacy with the Divine, it is not really possible for us to return to that terror. The love with Him drives the terror and it drives us back through the terror.

We do not accept and receive the love so that we do not have to feel. If we begin to accept the love, we may then question why we need to move through the feelings, the trauma. Intentionality is often seen as what we want to do, what is our own motivation.

But the deeper intentionality is the unconscious, unknown trauma that drives us to make choices that are compensatory.

But our compensatory choices still do not really cover up the terror. We come from being homeless (knowing we are no longer with the Divine) or from some degree of pain or fear or trauma or some terrible thing or some deeper knowing that we do not ever get back to. Intentionality is really reactions that have layered up from this base terror, reactions that are compensatory.

The deeper reason for why we do what we do is the initial trauma itself. When the deeper reason for doing things is the fear that something bad is going to happen, it is a projection of the deeper terror of something bad that did happen. Maybe it happened when we were two and realized God was not here and there was no one here to protect us. If we are not with the Divine, then everything we are and all of our motivations for doing "good" things may all go back to that original terror. The intention of intentionality is to not go back to the terror.

But the dreams want to take us back to the terror and through it, back through the feeling to find the Divine.

THE "ADVANTAGE" OF NIHILISM

The whole "advantage" of being nihilistic is that we are not open to the pain and the vulnerability required to receive the pain. We prefer not to be open because then we can control. We can take a knife and stab ourselves in the back. We can be angry. It is our choice.

In a way, nihilism consumes us and we do not even feel we are in control of it. But when given the opportunity to return to a place of nakedness and vulnerability, we will find it very hard to be that exposed. When we are nihilistic, we are not exposed. We do not get any love, but we are also not exposed.

When is it preferable to not be exposed? We find it preferable the second we lose our connection with the child self. Instead of being exposed, we learn to be angry or in control or charming or sweet or carefree. Of course, if we jump away from our vulnerability, then we do not have to feel pain or love or true ecstasy or true passion or true fear. The whole myriad of feeling is lost to us. Most of us do not miss it. Most of us, if given the chance to feel, do not want to feel.

It is a failing of humanity that we choose to not feel and then believe that emotions are feelings. We believe emotions are feelings because our egos can engage in them. Then we can have this force of personality that flies through the feelings. Why would a rage-a-holic or someone who takes lithium to suppress emotional rage stop taking these drugs? Because they become numb in those places.

We will stop, will come off the drugs because we want to feel something. If we cannot feel our real feelings then we will feel our emotions. And maybe some of those are real feelings that the therapist does not know how to help us channel so we can feel them. R.D. Laing talks about letting people that are "insane," go "crazy," in order to cycle through what they are feeling. We say the same thing.

But we would rather not be crazy. We do not trust our feelings to lead us out. We think we are going to end up being killers or lose our spouses or our jobs or everything. We are scared of the child self and all the feelings and primalcy of that child self.

Avoiding Fear Avoiding God

Fear occurs when we are separate from the Divine and separate from our feelings, our child self. Fear is the absence of knowledge. When we have fear, it is because we are not conscious.

Pretending we do not have fear is not the answer, for fear is actually the way through. When we have fear, we assume there is something wrong, that there is something evil. But fear can be just a portal to other things.

When we are afraid of the fear, then we give pathology power. But if the fear is simply the fear of the unknown, then we can stand in the fear and assume that there is something good behind the fear.

Does this mean we do not feel the fear? No. But we can feel the fear as the door rather than jumping away from it. We can give fear a chance.

If we encounter something we think of as evil in a dream, we could be afraid of it, but more likely, we are really repulsed by it. Most of us are not lost in evil, we are just manipulated by it. When we see it in a dream, we can see it as repulsive and ridiculous.

Like in the Harry Potter book series, when the boggart comes out of the closet as the scariest thing the person can think of, the way to battle it was to say "Riddikulus." Then, the thing would disappear.

Evil only can exist where there's separation from the Divine. Evil does exist, but it does not really exist when we are with the Divine.

When we are faced with something that seems evil in a dream, we must stand in our fear and face what it is. It may be the goodness of creation. But when we are afraid, we often have misguided faith or no faith at all. In the process of avoiding our fear, we avoid God. The Divine is terrifying but in an awesome sense, in the way that terrifying is good. When we meet our maker, we are scared. It is frightening to face the Animus.

This is the fear of facing the unknown, the mystery, what is more powerful than us. We do things to induce fear in this way – there are those of us who climb mountains, skydive, do extreme sports. Why? Because we challenge ourselves to feel fear. It is a rush.

This work is about fear, too, because it works for us. This is not to say, "Go and do extreme sports. Jump out of a plane!" But, if there is a dream about jumping out of a plane, then the work would be to face into the fear of jumping, and jump.

It is facing the fear with integrity – being willing to trust and be open to what we cannot control. Ultimately, letting go of control is a form of dying, which always creates fear. Our control is how we are in the way of being with the Divine.

We need to break what we feel attached to, that we control. We control so that all hell will not break loose. But hell has broken loose. When we do not know this, we believe that we can control our own lives and make it all better.

Most of us wait to face this when we are facing death. But why wait? Why wait until we have no control to have no control? We have no control anyway. This is the challenge of facing into our worst fears.

Our Feelings Belong to Us

The pathology gets stronger when we deny something wonderful. It is amazing how it feeds on our beauty. It feeds on our desire for devotion but it feeds on it through projection. Once the desire to devote - to be loved and to love - gets projected into the world, onto the imperfection where it can never really be fulfilled, then the pathology flourishes. Like mold. All the ingredients are there.

If we go back to the wound instead of projecting it – back through the dreams uncovering layer after layer of what was wounded and left behind, left for dead - then the projection stops and the pathology cannot function in the way it has. It may turn and attack us for it. But we can get through this too, if we are willing to feel our feelings.

The alchemy of that capacity to feel the feelings will then emerge so the Archetype can work with those feelings. As long as we maintain that capacity by feeling it as our own loss. We can get to the place where we say our wound happened at a specific moment in out lives, and also that it does not really matter because we all lose our way anyway.

Maybe it would have been helpful if we had loving

people around us but why bemoan that fact? To clean it all up is not about being good. It is about finding the wound, finding the child that is in the wound. By feeling into the feelings of the wound, we become autonomous because our pain belongs to us.

Our fear belongs to us; our pain belongs to us. They are parts of how we, as divine beings, experience things. We need to follow the threads of the feelings in our dreams – which is difficult it brings us to the inside rather than to the place where we can project it onto the outside.

If we can get healed outside, then the healing comes on our own terms. We would much prefer things on our terms. But our terms are from a place of separation so how can it lead to anything really real?

As children, once we do not find the Divine in this world of suffering, pathology simply takes over. The child self regresses and disappears and we grow into lost adults, forever looking for our way back to ourselves. Once the child self is abandoned, what fills in the gap of its conscious existence is what we know as the human race. In a sense the human race is deprived of its soul.

Simply put, it could take our entire lives or it could only a few years, but the abandoned child in each of us is the way out of our suffering. The abandoned child is the way into our hearts and to our pain that will sooner or later be reflected back to us as the love that wants to heal that abandoned child.

But until we stand in that child, no matter what we do, even if we become a moral, upright and upstanding person, we will never be what we really are - that which is capable of receiving Divine love.

Stage Two

The Ego as a Field of Consciousness

The ego is necessary because it is a field of consciousness that evaluates, makes choices, is the center of free will. It is the center of consciousness. We need it.

Without it, we have no capacity for self-awareness. The problem with self-awareness, however, is that it becomes too preoccupied with itself. The ego's self-awareness becomes more important than God's perception of us. How God perceives us should be more of a concern than it is. We are so good at evaluating and deciding for ourselves whether we are okay or not okay, whether we hate ourselves or love ourselves, and so on. But this is not God's love. It is just opinions we make based on the criteria and the capability of our ego to feel certain ways and define itself in certain ways.

When feelings that come from the soul percolate up into consciousness, the ego will tend to transfer those feelings into some kind of creative act or expression, in the more fortunate personalities. These people are living in some kind of connection with themselves, but they are still not themselves. They take only some connection and bring it into a place where they can insert it into the world. They bring it back into gyroscopic relationship to others.

In other words, they can feel good or not good based on the acceptance or rejection of that part of themselves by the world. They can receive or not receive love based on this inner life.

People like this may feel into some vulnerable place and can reflect themselves through art, briefly delving into a sense of consciousness in order to bring it to the canvas or a poem or a story, for example. But the ego is still dominant. The part once brought to the surface of creative expression is gone. The minute it is put onto the canvas, the minute it is stated, whatever ambient feeling that is released from it is gone. All the person is left with is the separation within or the projecting into the world looking to fill the isolation/separation from the world.

We all do this in different ways, even those of us fortunate enough to have a creative connection with a part of ourselves. But it is dangerous as well. This is why there are artists who are corrupt, who are miserable, who cut off their ears like Vincent Van Gogh.

The insanity is simply the insanity of knowing too much and yet not enough, sensing into the Divine incarnate in the self and yet not being able to live it. The split is intolerable. The ego maintains that split, wants to keep that split because it has learned to identify itself as an expression of a self isolated from God or isolated from the soul.

Is this pathology? It is a good question. It may be our tendency to continue looking for ways to define the self as an automatic reflex to just being alive. Integratively speaking, we are always bringing material, even spiritual material, into consciousness, and the ego attempts to integrate it and make it something it can use.

Dying to Self is the opposite. The ego, in a way, does not die but becomes secondary to the incarnate soul in the self that is connected to God. When the ego is in control, it is like the tail wagging the dog. The ego tells us that if we let the soul out, the soul would be the tail wagging the dog. The ego is frightened to allow a part of the self out that we only let out in bits and pieces if at all. If we even know it exists.

When we die to self, we die to that soul, that incarnate essence of soul.

When we die to self, we let that soul become the most powerful thing in the psyche. Of course, the soul has its own problems because it is not perfect. It is like a child, needing support from God. It needs corrections and direction.

This makes becoming connected to the soul and having support from the Divine for that soul a complicated issue since we are raised in a world where there was no support, where we learned shame.

It is quite a division the ego needs to maintain or believes it needs to maintain for its own sense of autonomy. The idea of the Prodigal Son/Daughter returning home means that the ego self has become regressive and the child self is taking over. Returning home is only possible when the soul has returned.

The Memory Pain Carries

Pain carries the memory of the time when we were innocent. In that place of innocence, we remember being loved – somewhere, we were loved. If we did not remember this love, we would not feel pain.

Our pain is what is left over of the memory of being loved somewhere back in time. We knew love – then we were rejected and we repressed the pain, which left us with nothing but personality functions. By remembering the pain, we remember the part that was hurt and deserved to be loved.

I had a client who was feeling pain in a dream with several women who were loving her. When we worked with the moment in the dream, she went into her pain and asked, "Why did you not love me, Mom?" This is actually a correct question. The question not for the women in the dream because they were not rejecting her – she was projecting onto them the rejection from her mother. But she was right to say and feel her pain around her mother. Her memory of separation from God goes back to her mother's rejection, so she needed to feel that pain. In this place, she knew she deserved to be loved.

We all were loved; we all were begotten by love. Every living thing was begotten in love. Part of the energy that is in all things is about love. Every living thing knows that love.

Humans certainly know when they do not have it. The development of self-awareness means that we respond reflexively to our surroundings on a feeling level when we suddenly feel the love taken away. When we feel this, we feel our hurt.

This is the immediate kind of ameba-like reaction. If an ameba or any living creature is hurt or threatened, it pulls back. All things need support, and when they do not get enough of it, bad things happened.

We came into this life, as all living things do, with the memory of being loved. All the damage did not happen with the rejecting mother or the rejecting father. We already were wounded when we came in. The mother or father just reinforced it. We do not even need to know about the wound that we came in with – the only thing that matters is for us to simply feel the feelings and the healing will come.

But the risk is great. For many of us remember that when we were open, we were rejected.

Self-Awareness and the Awareness of God

Becoming self-aware means becoming separate from God. If we are aware of ourselves, we cannot be aware of God because we cannot be aware of both at the same time. The only place this could happen is in heaven, whatever that may be. But when we are born, our self-awareness is without God.

We are all terrified because of this. Those of us who can manage with this terror tend to function better in the world by suppressing our anxiety. But the better we are at managing, the farther away we are from God. It takes the anxiety to deal with the self-awareness of our separation from the Divine. Without the anxiety, we are not really self-aware.

Ironically, it is the anxiety that allows us to be self-aware.

Our job becomes finding God in this consciousness, and the place to start is the anxiety. The anxiety is there because we need to find God. The anxiety may say many things about our fears based on our life experiences, but the root of the anxiety is that we do not know our relationship with God. Without our relationship with God, we are lost.

To get back to that relationship, we have to feel the anxiety. It is tinged with pain because the loss of self and the loss of God is painful. Anxiety and pain go together. Feeling them together can be a doorway to self-discovery and discovering our relationship with the Divine. This is how we are when we are children. Every child feels it.

Of course, the question and experience of God is what God means to each individual. The only important experience is our own, based on our relationship with the Divine and who we are in terms of that relationship.

In an abstract, esoteric understanding of the Divine, there is no real place for us, for the individual. The power of dreams is that the Archetype is always focused on the intimacy with us, the uniqueness of that intimacy. In this way, the experience of God is not an abstract idea; it is an actual experience of love, of direction, of belongingness that is unique.

This is the only knowing that is worth knowing.

When we try to relate to God as a concept or as a belief, it is just a word. But when we encounter some aspect of the Divine in our dream life or in our outer world, then those questions are answered. When we have an experience, it is an experience. There is no discussion or theorizing because it just is.

We live the grace if we are deep enough in our work to have an encounter with the Divine in a dream. We experience this more in our dream life because we are more open to our unconscious and the Divine when we are asleep.

When we have that experience, this is what we want to live for until the next dream with an even deeper experience with the Divine. These are the experience for me that I just want to drink from. When I am drunk with them, I do not really care about the other questions because they are simply intellectual

There is no feeling, no experience to the concept of God, the concept that God created everything. But there is a feeling and an experience when we encounter God in our dreams – feelings of joy and pleasure and love. Even of pain and fear.

The feeling and experience is far more satisfying than understanding that God is the creator of all things. In that concept, there is the concept of being good to be with God, which is dry and tyrannical.

In the Adequacy

In the adequacy means being in His love. We always want to go back to our precondition because there is something about the love or feeling good in relationship to Him that is terrifying. It is true that we have trauma and that we hold on to control, but the journey of the dark night of the soul is the journey down, and it also goes against some part of us that does not want to go.

Of course, the pathology does not want us to go, but there is also some part of us that does not want to go. Some part of the ego is consciously scared of going because there is something in the revelation that is more than just feeling His love.

We talk about His love, how great it is. And it is. But we rarely get to the obvious question – if His love is so great, why are we so scared? We see it as a human condition that we are scared because when we are faced with God, it is too overwhelming to take in.

But what does this mean? The reality is so much larger than we are capable of understanding. We live in a world where we feel lost, isolated and where we have to control things. We have acclimated to it. Add to this the way we create our own order – we are gods in our own insanity.

And we use God to create order. We pray, we look to philosophies and to religion to create order. But this is not His order. It is our created order. This is the biggest lie of all – that we believe we are learning about God's ways.

The dream tells us the truth. If we are using God to create order, if we are using God's love to create order, then it is not God's love. There may be an idea of God's love, and there may even be some love in it, but it is not God's love. God's love means giving up our order, the order we create that may even be utilizing God's love or even the lack of God's love. Either way, the order we create is not God's love. Either way, we are faced with the reality that there is an order in the universe and we do not have a clue.

And yet. We are offered the gift to be part of it in a way that we have not been offered in our entire lives. This is the first condition of a calling – the desire to go on the journey. The second condition is being offered the calling. It is important to know that part of being offered our calling is being able to stand in the fear of it even though it is nothing but glory. This is not about trauma, but about beholding the miracle. What is revelation but things revealed?

But things that are revealed to be revelatory must be things that are terrifying.

It is much nobler to say that we are traumatized and so cannot look than to say that we are no longer traumatized and that we are just plain scared to look. This is the choice. We can use trauma as an excuse. There are those who are transcending trauma but who literally hold on to the trauma as an excuse not to go to the deeper fear, the Archetypal fear. To not look into the unknown. It is easier to use trauma as an excuse when called because if we say yes, then something is going to be asked. We are afraid of what is going to be asked, or we are afraid of the whole power of the Divine being at our doorstep.

What was it for Moses when he saw the burning bush? He did not understand what happened for he went down off the mountain and went into a rage at the people. If he had really understood, he would not have gone into a rage. God does not get mad and punish. We punish ourselves with our ignorance. The problem with Moses is not that God punished him, but that he never got it. It was too big for him.

Noah, however, built an ark and he built it in a desert. He stands out from all the different religious texts as a character, for he is a mortal man who beholds the miracle and simply accepts it. Simply is obedient. Not blindly obedient the way Moses was, but obedient.

God saved the world for one man. He did not save the world for Moses. He saved the world for Noah. Noah never beheld a burning bush for he never needed the flash of God. He did not need the image. God gave Moses the flash, the image, because Moses could never get it.

The burning bush is our hearts. Our immortal hearts.

Moses thought outside of himself, so God gave him the burning bush. But Noah was inside. The burning bush is inside all of us, burning like a beacon, calling us to the Divine. This is what we are afraid of.

The burning bush is not just the Divine love; it is the burning of our hearts and the calling to an enlightened state in which we become like Noah. But who wants to be Noah? We usually do not want to be anybody but our own lost selves because we believe it is safer to stay in our own reality, perpetuating some accommodation that makes us comfortable. We are comfortable in our suffering and uncomfortable in the potential promise.

But more is better. When we say yes to what He offers, it is simply a blessing. What are we afraid of? Everything. If we can stand in that fear of everything, we can be in the glory.

Women and Men

I have a painting of a woman looking to her husband while the husband is playing a horn and looking toward heaven, toward God.

This image portrays the idea that men look to God for their sense of worth and women look to men. It is an old idea, an idyllic way of understanding the relationship between men and women. A way that has been prevalent in most cultures and most religions.

But the reality is that men do not really look to God at all. Men look for structure, rules, the outline, the goal. Men look for the guidance in words – the Torah, the Koran, the New Testament, the Bhagavad Gita, and on and on. When men look to heaven, they are not really looking to heaven, but for a rule book they can call heaven.

But God is about feeling and love. To have that love with God, we must be in right relationship with ourselves. We have to be broken to the child.

In truth, men are really seeking women. When no one is looking, there is an affair happening, a tryst, a longing. Men have tried many ways to castrate this urge through celibacy, but the urge has not been easily squashed.

The urge is actually misunderstood. The urge is not really an urge for women; this is just a psychological problem that can be worked through. This urge is also a spiritual problem. In truth, men are seeking women all the time. Jung and Freud both knew this. There is no way of breaking it.

The Wandering Jew by Eugene Sue opens with a one-page story of a man and a woman travelling from two different directions to the top of the world, supposedly in order to find God. But when they meet, facing each other across a small expanse of water, he falls on his knees and reaches his arms not to God, but to the woman. The woman, however, points to heaven.

It is the woman who points to heaven. This is the Valkyrie, the Girl, the woman warrior who pulls the dying men from the battle and brings them to Valhalla, the great hall of Odin, to heaven. To God. It is the feminine principle that points the way to the male principle, not the other way around.

This does not mean that women know the answer; it just means that men do not know the answer but they pretend to and they pretend to be the ones in authority. The men pretend to be the ones who know God. But what men really want is a warm bosom to rest their weary heads upon. If men claim closeness to God, maybe they feel they deserve the right to have that warm bosom.

The woman points to heaven. She encourages the man to seek the Father, to lose his wanderlust. The Wandering Jew is about people who seek God and never find Him. Who seek God without seeking God.

God does not exist as a goal to be found. God exists as the absence of all goals. The child has no goal; it only knows it wants to be loved. There is nothing to prove, no mountain to climb, no revelation to be known, no problem to be solved. The child just wants to be loved. When the man comes home to the woman, he just wants to be loved.

When the man comes to the woman who is a Valkyrie, she points to the Father and her heart exclaims, "You are very close now because you found me. Just a few more steps and you will be home." For when the man walks in his Father's house, he does not return as the conquering hero; he returns as the child.

He is not looking for the salve that the mother would put on his wounds; he just wants his Father's love. The woman knows this, but the man does not. It is the woman who points to heaven.

In the story in *The Wandering Jew*, the man wanders throughout the world, finding nothing. In his wanderings, he comes to the end and gives up. At that moment of giving up, he faces into the power of the Father, which is the storm raging around him. He is weary, tired, vulnerable. Only then is he ready to return home.

The greater the love, the less any of it matters – different views of the world, of God, are not just normal but good. If love is in play, then the differences are irrelevant. If we really feel the love, then all the views lead us to the same place.

Projecting onto the Animus

People evaluate the Animus based on their dysfunctional relationships with the men in their lives or with their own dysfunctional male side. Even Jungians get confused on the notion that the internal projection of whatever is inside onto men outside is what the Animus is.

This is exactly what the Animus is not. The dreams reflect how women who are wounded project the things that would hurt them onto men, or how those who have a positive Animus place in themselves will seek support.

Either way, it is always projection and it is always in the world. The Animus wants to be known as himself – whether we have positive Animus projections and positive male experiences or negative ones. The Archetype is always inside – wanting to reflect itself on its terms and not through projection into the world.

This is a very confusing issue for psychologists and Jungians who reflect Animus in terms of their own criteria, their own intellect, their own dysfunction rather than any encounter with Animus. Then it becomes a self-fulfilling prophesy. Women choose men who will cause the wound that they have already experienced.

But that is not Animus. This is merely the projection of memories and experiences and trauma with men or with the father or even with the mother. Who knows how far back these experiences go? But the primary Archetypes, the ones at the bottom of the sea, at the bottom of the deepest core, the Animus and Anima, have their own integrity that has been lost to us.

It is hard for the Archetypes to reach us if we are living in projections of our own misery, our memories of whatever happened to us over the millennium. How do we cut through this if we are continuously projecting instead of going deep down inside to see what is – what is hurt and what is pain and what are bad experiences – so we can differentiate them from the pure form of the Divine.

It can also be pathological when we have a "good" projection onto the Animus, when we have good memories of the male and things in our outer lives. As long as we are projecting, it is difficult for the Archetypes to reach us.

When the Animus and that deep unconscious touches us, what arises is the pure form of Divine love. We experience this reality through our deepest hurt. Then all that source of the projection – our deepest hurts – can be ameliorated and we can live the inner connection to the Divine in our outer consciousness.

Then the Animus can really live within us.

Women and the Animus

Women can stay above ground and become goddesses like Psyche, living in the twilight of the self-made beautiful life, or they can enter their woundedness and face into the man of their dreams, the way Persephone entered into the Underworld.

The Animus is the man. Somewhere inside, most women know the Animus is the man who loves them more than anything. But most woman have already given that up. Cupid's arrow strikes, poisoning with love. Then, the woman does not want to go into the deep well.

We have all been hurt. Most women have been hurt by relationship and they learn that they cannot trust men, that they cannot trust anything with a penis. We hear, "Do not love, do not trust love, do not trust the feelings of attraction or passion for the Animus."

If a woman does feel that passion, she must go into the well, into what is underneath. When we learn that facing into our passion hurts, we wonder why we would do it.

The Animus is not like any other man – women must be clear that the only thing a man has in common with the Animus is a penis. That is all. If a woman does not trust men, she will not want to have anything to do with the Animus.

When a woman is first entered by a man, there is blood. There is woundedness in the very act of being entered when she makes love with a man she loves. But the man is not the Divine.

When the Animus reenters the woman, she is wounded all over again but this time the wound comes from knowing that she is loved. Finally, truly loved. The pain, the drop of blood, the tear-drop is called the secret of the pomegranate because it is the recognition of the love lost and found again.

Women who are content to be goddesses are content to remain above ground in the world. But there are those who are called to this deeper yearning. These are ones who wish to be twice-born.

Pathology can use this yearning, of course, to create false spirituality, an aesthetic spirituality, in order to create a conflict. But there is already a conflict in us about our deeper spirituality. The conflict is recreated or created in a new way in order for us to see that what may be spiritually satisfying or may seem good/evil is at odds with the outer world.

This split carries all the pain and the separation of another, deeper split. We have to go down to our souls, down into the ground. It is about going deep inside to find ourselves so that we can be with the Animus.

The soul is always buried underneath the ego, it is always in the unconscious. Persephone descends to find not just the Animus, but to find her self.

Getting Affirmed by the Animus or Affirming the Child

When we are looking for and needing affirmation from the Animus in a dream and the Animus is there to give that affirmation in a positive way, a counter dream may come where there is no Animus and we are affirming the child.

Would we rather receive the affirmation from the Animus or give the affirmation to the child. It is a great deal easier to give affirmation than to receive affirmation because it is so much more vulnerable to receive. To receive from the Animus as a child is very difficult to do after we have grown into adults.

All that we have formed, our sense of identity, all the ways we have coped and managed, would suddenly have to cease to exist in order for us to be the unformed child who is being loved by the Animus. This is why in Alchemy, we die to the child so that we can be loved by the Animus – it is required that we lose all in order to be the receiving child.

Without the soul, there is no love. The ego tries its best with what it has, but it does not get the love because it is without the soul. It just has the love it accumulates in itself, the kind of love that is finite and limited.

ABUNDANCE

Abundance in a dream is not just about abundance, but about understanding that when we are in an impoverished state – really, the normal state of the world – we often feel as if we have to make everything happen. The abundance shown to us in a dream is to show us that the Divine is here and can do anything it wants. It has access to every drop of oil, every drop of water, every dollar, all the food, every miracle – everything.

Just as pathology does.

The Divine has access to all the material world because it lives in two dimensions. And, like pathology, the Divine can do anything it wants in the world if we cooperate. It can make whatever happens, happen.

Our prayers do not make it happen.

Which may seem disappointing. But people really pray so that they do not have to dies to self. The real prayer is becoming the child self, the boy, the girl. We pray when we do not have a connection, for it is an attempt to find the connection. God may or may not respond, but the issue really is that most of us are not our child, soul self when we pray.

In a dream with never-ending food, for example, it

means that the Divine is never-ending. All the obstacles we witness in the world – financial and emotional obstacles – are just illusions. When we are with Him, there are no obstacles. When we are the child self with the Father, with the Animus, there are no obstructions. This is what abundance teaches and the dreams is showing that we can feel and live that reality.

But we cannot just train our mind. We have to become the thing – we have to become the child. What child who has been loved properly does not believe in Santa Claus, does not have hope, does not belive that he or she is going to be completely cared for. This knowing that only a child can have, this innocent knowing and faith in God, faith in being loved and taken care of, this is how we came into the world.

This is the part of us that needs to come back. The child brings all the knowing that the Divine is here, is in our lives. The child know that all his or her prayers are being answered and really there is no need for prayer. Being the child is being a prayer.

Choosing the child or thinking of being the child is not the same as being the child. In a dream about abundance, the child self is not surprised, is not shocked. There is endless peace for the child self, endless possibility.

The reality of the child self is this possibility, this abundance. It is not the reality in which we were raised, not how we see the world, not how the world treats us. This is all illussion. We all conspire together in our misery to believe a certain thing, then we try to grab for our piece of it so that there is not enough for everyone.

For the child, this reality does not exist. What is true is that God supplies the abundance and the blessing for the child.

But we have to go into our dark night of the soul, we have to enter into our own valley of the shadow of death. This dying to self that then leads to the mercy and goodness that will follow us all the rest of our days. That mercy and goodness is for the child. We have the dark night of the soul so that we will die and the child self will live. The child's innocence, belief and knowing God can be the light of our lives, is our innocence.

FALLING, FALLING, FALLING

Why do we have images of falling in dreams? Because the foundation of the self is actually much deeper than what we know. Our gyroscopy manages the self so we create a sense of – or a paradigm of – what we are. We create a kind of a structure that has a bottom and a top and a side. We create walls and a floor and a ceiling that is our ego self.

When we leave our ego self – since there is no way to find out real selves unless we leave it – we have falling or drowning dreams. These kinds of dreams are about letting go of some concept or some way we know ourselves.

We believe that if we fall, there will be no bottom. There is no bottom that we are aware of.

There is a bottom somewhere, a basis for being supported. But in the falling, we feel that there is no support and that we are falling to certain death. If we can pass through the fear, we can realize there is a bottom, there is support – just not in the way we know it.

Falling typically means falling into the illusion that there is nothing. Falling into the fear of nothing. The fear of nothing is really the fear of leaving who we are and engaging the mystery of the self we do not know.

The universe always surprises us. Every time we create a paradigm of the physics of the universe, new scientific breakthroughs – which occur almost daily now – show us that the universe is not what we thought. The universe does not act the way we thought, and neither does the human psyche. This is the world we live in now – poised for evolution. We are all poised for something greater.

It is not enough to observe it in the mind through science; we have to find it in ourselves. Because we are the stuff of the universe. Carl Sagan said, "We are made of star stuff," meaning the material of stars, but I would say we are of the universe.

In our souls, in the door of ourselves, we are identical to the universe. The soul is linked to the beginning of the universe. We are the same reality – it is the reality in the reality. There is the physical seen universe and there is the unseen universe, which we now call dark matter.

Dark matter is forces working in the universe that cannot be seen, but can actually be found (based on the effects on visible matter around it). These invisible forces actually have more effect on how the universe behaves than any known physical law. This quantum leap in science becomes a quantum leap in this work, as well.

What we hold on to is nothing, and what we fear is nothing is really everything. It is all reversed. This is the trick we live in, until we can break it. But we cannot break it with our minds. We have to break it by feeling. The dreams do not tolerate mental understanding.

The important issue in falling is what we let go of, not just where we are going. We let go of the self that needs to die, the self that is not of the soul. When we fall, we free fall into the night – into the dark night of the soul. The dark night is where the Archetypes can support us.

There are times when we must make the choice to fall or not to fall. Free will. No one can make us fall. If the Archetype in a dream made us fall, without our choosing to fall, then our will would still be intact.

Choosing not to fall is a learning, too. When we choose not to fall, we can then see how we are still holding on, exposing pathology. For, are we holding on, or is it the pathology in us that wants us to hold on?

If we are aligned with pathology, if we are clear that we do not want to hold on, then we can let go. It is our choice. If we decide not to let go, then we suffer the decision to hold on to the pathology that wants us to hold on.

Into the Darkness to Reach the Light

When we get to the center of the storm, into the deepest part of the well and then get through it, the dark well water opens up to white light. It is like being in a tunnel and seeing an opening at the end.

When we are at that opening, we look back at where we have come from and what we see is nothing but all the lies and all the projections onto the world. We see everything that made us think it was all about everyone else.

In that moment, we realize that it was always us. It was our projection of hurts or fears, so that, in a way, everything in the world was self-created. Yes, there may be mean people in our lives or we may have had terrible parents or some things we could not control, certainly. But so much of it is determined by what we create through our projections.

When we are on one side of the tunnel and we do not see the light, we always think that whatever we feel is somehow related to the world around us. We think that it is not about us at all. We are in our arrogance or our unworthiness. But ultimately, it is all based upon some judgment or something that is projected into the world that we do not even understand.

The deeper feelings are not even touched. In the midst of that, we are in a state of purgatory of trying to figure out who we are or finding a place of safety from the confusion. We become paralyzed in our own pathology, our own sweat. The very thing we create to protect ourselves becomes the very thing devouring us, and we do not know it. It is like a parasite tricking us to let it devour us like some terrible nightmare we never awaken from.

Undoing that means first waking up to the reality that, rightly or wrongly, we may believe we are better off not even knowing about the nightmare we are living. There is something in us that says, "Hey, if I do not know about it, I will not have to deal with any of it."

In a way, this is a good strategy. We will never get to the light but, we will never have to face the nightmare. Most of us do not live anywhere near the nightmare of ourselves. We live in this protracted projection where we have made everything seem nice. Who wants to tamper with that?

Yet, we can undo all of the mechanisms we have created to make it all right to be alive by getting to the nightmare of how we have been. When we can see that, we can get to the deeper, real love.

Innocence Under the Scab

Trauma takes a moment when we are in a place of innocence and nakedness and then, in that moment, something happens - there is an ambient emotional reality that suddenly inserts a dark cloud into that innocent moment. Rather than being able to manage the moment and carry the innocence along with the threat, the innocence is repressed to repress the threat. Everything, including our innocence and our connection, gets pushed away.

If, as children, we were able to stay in the threat, in that moment, and not run away, the wound would not be as deeply buried. In this case, the trauma is not as deep; we carry it on the surface. The moment still creates neurosis and is projectable, but at least we have all the pieces. The pieces are fear, the wound and some of our innocence – all of which are tied up in our consciousness or subconsciousness.

But when we cannot tolerate any of our feelings, then the innocence – which is the part of us that feels those feelings – is repressed along with the uncomfortable feelings. When this happens, a vacuum is created, causing a great deal of damage to the psyche. The deep well is pushed way down deep, and the rest of the psyche builds material on top of that well, which is not authentic.

This material is like a scab. It is not based on the innocence and truth of our vulnerability but on what we use to cover the trauma and cope. To reclaim all of this means remembering those feelings, which is exactly what we want to do the least.

Ironically, underneath those difficult feelings is the innocence, where we can feel love and trust and openness. This is the place before the damage happened, where we can once again find Divine love.

But we cannot find the Divine love if we suppress our wound. The wound is the place of our innocence and the place of our capacity to receive. From this place, we can seek Divine love whenever the fear or uncertainty comes up, rather than pushing the whole thing away.

Balance of the Archetypal Mother and Father

When a daughter seeks her mother's love – even though her mother has not bonded with her and she bonds with the mother who does not love her – the daughter has to give up all her feelings and all her pain to excuse the mother of her rejection.

In so doing, such a woman seals the door to her own ability to create because she cannot accept her own feelings. This is catastrophic to the female soul because, in this case, the mother is more important than the daughter. This scenario drops the child self, the soul self, the clitoris self to the deepest levels of repression.

Women who love mothers who do not love them and who do not know that their mothers do not love them become deeply lost in lie after lie. They have to repress so much of what they feel in order to maintain the relationship with the mother. It is utterly crippling. This is the most devastating example of loss of creativity. Women who are wounded in this way often become compulsive and preoccupied with things that have nothing to do with themselves,

We need to rectify the balancing act we maintained with the mother in order to return to a deeper reality where the soul self lives in harmony with the Mother and the Father. In the Archetypal Realm there is no such infraction. For any of us reconnect to our soul, any dysfunction, any lack of harmony, any way we have compensated for the lack of harmony and balance, even if is "successful," still will not work in the Archetypal Realm.

Because the child never needed to rectify the problem in the first place. It simply disappeared. It simply dropped out of sight and maintained herself in a perfected state underneath consciousness waiting for the time for the imbalance to be addressed. Whether it is a positive imbalance that is a healthier way we have coped or not, the imbalance still needs to change to the perfect state in which the child experiences reality archetypally.

Being with the Son, Not the Father

The goal of the work is not to be with the Father. The goal is to be with the Son, the Animus. The Animus is the liaison between the two because we can never really know the Father.

The spiritual Father is too big – we have no understanding of God because we are too small to understand Him. The best way we have to understand God is through the projection onto the father. The father, who is objectified outside of us, is the closest thing to God that we can understand.

The mother is objectified inside of us; we come from inside the mother. The mother is the earth, the power of our natural selves. It is in the psychological where God is the highest. God is the highest of high, the highest knowing that is beyond knowing.

God is not really the father. It is just the way that we consecrated that understanding when we were children – our fathers seemed awfully big and distant to us and so the father becomes that. The wound with the father reflects itself in some way on the Divine that is unknowable.

But we can know the Animus. The Animus knows the Divine more than we do and also knows us more than we do. The reason for being with the Father is a way to get to the Son, a way back to the Animus, back to the Angel of Mercy. The Animus exists between those two realms – He has the love of the Divine and He reflects it back to us.

If we have father issues, particularly for men, the idea of going back to the father is simply to break the ego. To let the worldly ego die so that we can then be with the Son, the Son who is already with the Father. The Animus is already with the Father when we come to the Father, and so we can be with Him.

For men, coming home to the Father heals the wound we have with our fathers and returns us to the innocent boys we were. Again, this is not the core issue, for the real alignment is with the Animus, the relationship we can have. We cannot have a relationship with the Father as it is God. We can have a father, but he is only the door to the Animus. From the psychospiritual realm, the Father plays a role of healing, but in no way does the Father reflect the larger meaning of God.

This is why there are two fathers in Greek mythology – Uranus and Cronus. The Cronus father is akin to our natural father and his son, Zeus, kills him through the mother. The Uranian father is the father that Cronus killed. The father dying to a father is the manifestation of something spiritually unknowable being brought into an intellectual realm. A construct of knowing that requires a deadening of understanding in order to know it in the mind. The idea of the son killing the father, as in Cronus killing Uranus, is a misnomer. Cronus never killed the father. It was just a way of bringing spiritual life into a more mortal realm of the physical.

In other words, to know the love and to transcend rules for many is unknowable. We have to come into our feelings. To do this, we must die to self so that which is not Divine in us can die.

We die to the child self and know essence from a place of what we really are and what we really were given – the spiritual soul self that has the right to re-exist in the world. That is what this path is all about.

We cannot have relationship with the Animus if we are poisoned by the mother, particularly for men. This is true for women as well, but in the male psyche, the way to correct the poisoning of the mother is through realignment with the Father. This realignment and Alchemy opens us to the innocence of self that allows us to be reclaimed by the Animus and Anima. The Animus and Anima are not parental; they are present in the Divine grace so that we can partner with them. More, they are like siblings.

When we partner with them, we work in the fields of Abraham, with Abraham being the psychological father. In the alchemical process, the man is with his brother, the Animus. Of course, the Animus knows more than the man – He is smarter and faster and knows more – but He is the brother. He is not the genesis of the love of the universe, but He is a vessel that receives the love. And He shows us that we can be a vessel, too.

Once we have healed the wound with our fathers, we can be open to the Father and we can be vessels as well. But we cannot be a vessel directly to the Divine. We receive the love through the Animus and the Anima.

When men do become the son of the Father, however, they often will compete with the other Son. If the Animus is more like a brother, then this competition aspect must also be broken. So, if we are competitive with other men, then we are competitive with the Animus by definition.

Part of the healing with the Father is the capacity to be more one with ourselves and connected with the disparate parts inside that we can then take ownership of. The reason we are lost from the Father is that we are really lost from ourselves. The break from the Father is really just a reflection of this. The shards of glass of the fractured mirror are what make us not able to see the wellspring of reality because we are too shattered.

Something that is shattered is the opposite of what is whole. When we are shattered, we do not understand wholeness.

When we become more whole, when aspects of ourselves are reunited, we can understand God or the Divine or wholeness or the essential focus of love. We can understand the beam of light that is the Divine spark that we lose when we are shattered. The Divine spark then is part of the shattering, and we project it onto people and situations. We look for love from women, from men, from anything. The more we project, the more the ego is shattered, the more the shards are out in the world.

When we withdraw the projections, we are taking these shards of glass, these shards of consciousness, and bringing them back into ourselves. This includes the pain, the fear, the hurt, but they can be worked through. The mystery of consciousness is always salvageable and solvable if we own it. It is never solvable if it is projected out into the world.

Once we pull it all back into ourselves, we can find the love of the Divine and eventually become autonomous. We can never be the vessel of love if we are split into two or four or ten or twenty.

When we come back to our soul self, come back to who we are, we become the vessel. Not a broken vessel, not a shattered vessel, but a vessel that can hold the love. This is the job of the soul: to hold the love. To hold the love, it must be itself whole.

Finding Versus Believing

When we are born into a world where there is no love, we have to create an identity. We all really want to do the right thing, even thieves. We all have a sense of correctness somewhere within us. Whether that sense is wrong or right, there is something in us that wants to be right.

Through this, pathology can manipulates us, or we can try to find role models that have the integrity that we have lost. But our role models do not have the integrity – we project what we have lost. And we can project this onto anybody, even Adolph Hitler. Before the war and during the war, Hitler was not seen as necessarily evil to some people. Some people believed in aspects of Hitler's cause as a way for German society to be free. The Germans were incredibly oppressed under the post–World War I peace agreement, and people could project that Hitler was striving to return them to glory.

A lot of dark things are done in the name of glory and in the name of love. Goodness, rightness, values—but they are not love. We confuse altruism with God's love, and we sometimes will go under the knife for something we believe. How noble, maybe heroic, maybe even right, but it is not love.

It is a different world when we bring love into the equation. Before we believe in anything, we have to find the Divine love. This is what we are being asked to do, to give up our sense of rightness and correctness, which sustained us as a being who did not have the love.

These values, these connectednesses cover up the tragedy, the fear, the isolation, the aloneness, the terror of not having love. By letting go of the need to be right, we can journey through that fear, the fear that, if left unfelt, begets worry and control.

If we stay in the fear, the Divine will come to us in that place where we were the lost child. That is how the work deepens itself. We can reconnect without all the compensations that we have had because there was nobody there.

He always was there. We were just too young to receive Him.

The world is really powerful when we are little children. Psychological work does not heal suffering; it reconciles it. Reconciling does not bring the Divine into our lives; it is simply another form of adaptation and working through without really becoming any different. We do not have to die to self; we just reconcile the problem and become a better manager to become a better high-functioning person. We may even have a better life, a happier life.

A better life is fine, but the goal of this work is to reclaim our souls and our lives in a Divine connection. This requires the descent into the darkest things that we carry so that they can be healed.

Deciding to Stay Open

When we are children, most of us are still open vessels. We feel things, we are sensitive, we have our own personalities. We have our own issues as kids, of course, but we have this place of really being open to the world, of being responsive to what other people do, to being loved, to being tickled, to being given a gift. We are like a flower and the sun is out.

But when things are bad, we have no tolerance. Children have no tolerance for abuse, but human beings have an enormous capacity for survival. It is why we are still on the planet even though we have lived the horrendous history of humankind. Up until the last sixty or seventy years, we lived in what we now consider to be a third world reality.

The lifespan of most people even in the 1940s was only forty-something years. This has doubled because the things that killed people back then do not kill people now. When the lifespan was forty, people did not really enough time to find the place of asking "Why am I here?"

When we are children, we are open but then we close down. We are here and then we are gone. There is no Santa Claus, no Animus, no God. We pray at church or at temple or at the mosque, but there is no real understanding of the Archetypal reality in this world. It is very hard to find.

We live the value of sweetness; we do not want to live *in* the sweetness. Because of this, most of us really feel the harsh edge inside of us coming at each other every day. If we are open, we are going to be stabbed constantly. People we care about simply turn on us for very little reason – maybe they had a bad day and they do not know it, so they blame us by finding something we have done. Or maybe they are jealous. We just never know.

As we come back to our child selves, not only are we coming back to our own trauma, but we are also re-exposing ourselves to more woundedness and more disappointments. But in that place where we expose ourselves to all of these things, we are also open to God's love and to an inner reality that through the work will unfold and give us support for being exposed. The support that we did not have as a child.

It is extremely difficult. We have to make the decision, a conscious decision, to stay open and be exposed to the wounding. We have to know that it is not generally deliberate, that no one is usually trying to hurt us, but that people are simply lost. When people are lost, they react. And we never know when the reaction is going to come. It is like navigating a field full of land mines. We never know when we are going to step on something or trigger something. It comes at us for no reason. The question is, Can we stay open to our vulnerable selves with the Divine even with all of this?

The decision to stay open is a big decision and it is understandable why people do not make that decision. When we go under and shut down, we are lost, we are separate, we are unreliable, unpredictable and dangerous. The decision is to not to go under and shut down but to work at becoming and staying open, connected and supported instead.

Part of this decision to stay open is to have it not come

from a place of survival, to not have it as part of our sense of identity or sense of coping, to not have it be a part of our will. Will is usually the will to survive, and the will to survive is coping. When we really surrender to Him, we do not need to use our will. It is a tough habit to let go of because it is who we think we are. If we take the "w" out of the word "will," then we are left with "ill." All will is ill will. But because the world is a dangerous place, our first question is, How can we survive without our will?

If we really know His presence and surrender our will to Him, we get truly supported.

The Need of the Child

The essence of every child is devotion. Every soul child loves its parents, loves God. It is innocent. It does not have an "I" that can rebel. It only has an "I" that can be hurt and wounded. It is the vulnerable self.

It is also very powerful because in devotion, the child has all the passion and all the colors of feeling – anger, pain, passion, creativity, surrender, obedience, all the way through love – it is all part of the devotion that comes from love.

Needing love, wanting love, needing to be loved, needing to love – the devotional person cannot be separated from the object of the devotion. This is supported in the image of the Madonna. This is the soul's rite of passage – to be supported and reinforced through the feminine.

This is why the mother is so important. To the degree that women are not devotional, children learn to be twisted out of their innocence. It does not mean the father does not have an effect, but when the mother is so close to the child, the child shares everything with her.

In this way, the child's ability to be a clear prism for love is compromised very early by the mother's inability to be in devotion and her struggles with men or other people or with herself. How the mother jumps away from her devotional side creates a separation.

The secret of the pomegranate is our core yearning for the Divine that gets lost. The secret of the pomegranate is the tear, is the wound, is the desire for God; it comes from the place of devotion. It is the clitoris; it is the girl. It is the feminine side that both women and men have. It is not about gender.

But men and women both have severe reactions to that level of innocence and vulnerability and passion and need. The essence of the soul is just that – essence, power, vulnerability and need. We all want to jump away from it because we have been hurt there. If we need, we get rejected. We have all learned to deny our need. Some get really angry, rebellious, belligerent; some become passive aggressive; some become broken to being a nothing, then follow somebody else. When we follow someone else from this place, this is a negative form of devotion. It is neediness, not autonomy.

The child knows what it is. The child needs out of the self, the autonomous self that is healthy. When we lose our child self, needing becomes pathology. Many of us associate devotion with neediness which is why we believe devotion is bad. When devotion is seen as pathological neediness, it means we are under someone else's control and abuse. When we are the child self, we are potent; when we are potent, we do not need someone who controls and/or abuses us.

The idea that being needy and vulnerable invites abuse is simply not true. Being needy and vulnerable is the place where we want the purest love. We would know the difference between pure love and abusive love, just as a child knows the beloved.

Many women react to vulnerability. They are afraid that if they become their vulnerable, feminine selves and care for a man, they will be abused. This is their belief around vulnerability from childhood.

But the true caring has already been lost. It has morphed into an adolescent caring that is not the same need for care that we felt as children. We take whatever is left of that need for care and project it into the world. We either get slammed or we are bored by the person who loves us. The only way out is to find and face into our vulnerability.

Vulnerability Breeds Potency

Vulnerability breeds potency. It allows for the Divine love to enter the vessel of the self. The reason for this is that when we are the state of vulnerability, we also feel pain. The precursor for love is pain; we cannot sustain the love without the pain.

But, if we put love and pain together as a function of reality, we find that we are either in the love or in the pain. Rather than being opposites, they are the same. When we feel this pain, we are in the Divine love and we are not lost. If we believe that being with the Divine is only about feeling love and we do not allow ourselves to have our pain, then we are going to jump away and back into our pathology.

We Must Matter

Selflessness and giving to others without God's love creates narcissism. If narcissism does not create tyrants, it creates martyrs. Martyrs are good tyrants – the difference is that the tyranny of their existence is that they go it alone. All in the name of love. Martyrs becomes bigger than God. They eclipse God.

Our heroes are martyrs.

The only way to really be a person that can give to the world and can love others is to first be the one that is loved. We have to become the Prodigal Son/Daughter; women have union with the Animus. Why? Because we must matter first.

To truly be in relationship with the Archetypes, we must matter. Otherwise, all the love we give comes back as martyrdom, which is a form of tyranny.

We can hide in a fear of being persecuted. The fear says, "Do not be the one. Do not stand with God." We try to find some way to manage. It is a difficult position – to be a person who wants to serve the world, help others while at the same hiding under a rock.

Persecution does not mean God abandoned us. Jesus was beaten and then nailed to the cross to die. God did not rescue him. But Jesus did not say, "There is no God." He did have his moment where he felt forsaken, saying, "My God, why have you forsaken me?" We all have that – it is part of the human condition. But Jesus moved through it; he did not stay with feeling abandoned. He moved to, "Forgive them, Father, for they know not what they do."

God cannot protect us completely – does he need to? If we truly have ultimate faith, we can suffer the consequences of our belief and not abandon God or feel abandoned by God. Just because the world betrays us does not mean God betrays us.

Many of us make this mistake – when the world does not treat us "right," we complain. We ask, "Why did God not do something?" We blame God for what other people do to us, as if God is supposed to rescue us or as if He is responsible for how people treat each other.

He is not. We are responsible for how we treat each other. But we make God responsible, and then blame Him.

Losing faith is a form of blame. The deepest faith is knowing that the most awful things can happen on this planet and it does not mean that God does not exist. The greatest faith is realizing that people are just lost and that we are destroying ourselves, that He is trying to help, but He cannot change our will. Only we can do that.

Point of Need

The point of need is not where we think we need, but the place where our soul self needs. When we face our death with integrity, it is a point of need, but the point of need could be really any moment in our lives where we are in our deepest selves. When our needs is aligned with our deepest selves, then the issues in our outer life are aligned, too.

Sometimes those needs reflect themselves as support in the world in a particular way, but always the root connection is to the soul.

If we are aligned with our souls, then all the external issues related to the deeper self create the possibility of the point of need. Of course, the point of need with the Animus is only one aspect of relationship with Him. There are many others – relationship itself, mutuality, fulfilling a calling, healing. But the point of need is the most personal aspect in the sense that the interior and exterior worlds are aligned so that the root connection of the soul and the external issues are also aligned.

Typically, they are not in alignment. When our concerns are different from our soul's concerns or His concerns, we are unlikely to get too much support. We may perceive we have a need such as getting something or making money or even having a certain person love us. But if it is not aligned with the interior world (and typically it is not, because it is too aligned with the world, without the soul), then it is not really a point of need.

Most prayers are not answered; our needs are aligned with the ego not the soul. It is a very esoteric to understand – one that becomes clear in the unfoldment of the soul self. We feel fulfillment around the issue of the point of need when we are aligned with our soul and not our ego.

When we begin to feel this alignment in our lives, we feel peace in whatever we do. The feeling of peace endures, whether we are facing death, a crisis in our life, the loss of someone we love, or some success. All of these areas are where the external and the internal combine with the connection to the Divine in a wonderful way where we feel this support.

An example would be a performer who is not uptight and nervous and caring what the audience thinks. Or if we are facing death, we have a peace about it because we know we have an immortal self. We feel the immortality of knowing that we continue beyond this life. This truth can be felt and known not through the mind, but through being touched and loved in our point of need.

In all things, the fundamental issue is that the presence of the Divine makes us understand how to find peace and love in any moment. In all things, He is there. Our point of need can be variable, and He will be there in the midst of it, as long as it is a true need and not a replacement for the Divine, something to help us in the outer world that is unrelated to the true need.

Obviously, we need to eat, we need money to pay our bills, and all those things, but if that need is disconnected from the more profound relationship with the Divine, it really may not answer the calling even though we think it should.

When we find our soul, we will find the support. He does not like to support us in our need in the world – He wants to support us in our need in our inner lives.

The Redemption of Pain

Since the story of being kicked out of the Garden of Eden, shame has been pathology's tonic for the dark mother to project onto the Father. The dark mother can say, "See? Your father hates you – he wants to eat you like Cronus ate his children."

When we get underneath the shame, there is a more vulnerable inadequacy that will allow us to feel the love of the Father. The problem is that pride wants to protect us from the shame or protect us from the vulnerability. Although there are other variations of pride that have to do with competition – like anger-based pride or fear-based pride – ultimately, pride always revolves around the mother on some pathological level.

The pathology's game is to protect us from the shame or from the vulnerability and insecurity with the father and ultimately, to protect us from the love of the Father. The pride says, "I am okay. I do not need any help."

There is some way pride powers the ego to survive no matter what suffering it is under. We might think this is a good thing, and it is – but it also blocks the love. It allows us to survive and it may allows us to be what we might call heroic.

And if pride does not work then shame will try to kill

us. And it does. There are people with very little pride, who have great shame and great self-doubt. They get attacked in a different way.

Pride empowers us, but it is really only on the surface levels. We cannot be in our souls when we are being empowered in this way.

Pain kills shame – not nihilism, but real pain. Pain also makes us aware of our need. Pain connects us with our inner self and from that place we can connect with the Divine – out of passion and need. Not out of shame or unworthiness or fear.

Pain is the ultimate vulnerability. It allows for forgiveness and it allows for redemption – meaning to reclaim what was taken. To reclaim the soul, to reclaim the consciousness, to reclaim the hope.

The True Pull of Gravity

For every action, there is an equal and opposite reaction. All of the actions that have happened since the beginning of time have caused reactions. These reactions are projections and reactions. Reactions cause other reactions which cause other reactions which cause other reactions and on and on. This is the world.

In this way, everything that ever was, becomes one big projection/reaction. This creates an inverted point. The world is a series of reactions that have actually filled up the physical plane with reactions and projections.

The inverse point, the descent through the deep well, takes us to the point before history. We are all going back to the big bang in ourselves, just as scientists are finding a way to go back in time to the universe's big bang by tracing gamma rays. Through this work, we return to the big bang in ourselves, to the place where creation began and then through all the reactivity from that point – all the history, all the lies, all the rape, all the horror, all the wounds.

When we go back to the beginning of time, through the deepest well, the deepest wound, we get to the beginning of creation. We get to the big bang, the spark, to that love that begat us all.

Each of us must journey to the dawn of our own time. Not the dawn of time, but our own time, to find that primalcy, that energy. Once we get to that, it is like going back to the past, back to immortality, back to the beginning of time. From this point, the child, the soul, can emerge in the world.

Instead of pathology flooding the world and flooding our psyches, what emerges in the world is all that "bangness," all that explosive energy, all that incredible love. And when we go back far enough, perhaps it is collective. We reach the place where it is the violation of us all. When we face our own death, we face the death of every person in the whole world. This is what makes good therapists of this work. If we fear our own death and our own pain, we cannot lead anyone else there.

God may have made us, but it is the terrible things that have happened to us that define us. Gravity, therefore, is what pulls us toward this history, toward this past – personal and collective. Gravity does not pull us toward God; it pulls us to our past. We cannot undo the past and find the Divine love if we do not face into the past.

Most aesthetic spirituality tells us that we simply look up to find God. The dreams tell us we need to look down. The belief is that if we look down, then we will be lost. If we face the monster, we will be lost. This is what horror movies show – the terror of the deep! Go deep enough into the ocean, into the jungle, into outer space and we will be devoured. The message is to not go deep – stay on the surface.

Do not go down those stairs. Do not go into the basement.

And yet, every night we sleep, the dreams attempt to bring us deeper or to show us how we are avoiding going deeper. The dreams reflect the gravity, the focus, the calling us back to that one moment of creation.

Gravity runs counter to everything we do because it is

the pull to our past. Because it is the pull to our past, it is also a pull toward God, but we have to face that past. It is the pull to the horror of horrors, to the dark night of the soul.

In that place stands the healing, the forgiveness, the redemption, for all humankind. All of us are damaged; all of us have a past that is hard to face. The dreams and dream therapists want to go underneath how we cope with it, underneath our desire to be "better" so that we are more functional or likable or noble.

The things that appear to be good and noble are as much a shallow grave as all the ignoble things we do. Aspiring to be noble is not the same as finding God. Being a good person is not the answer. The answer is the result of Divine living.

What do we see when we look in His eye? Our past; the horror of the past. We are afraid to look at that horror, and pathology uses that against us. But if we have the courage to look at the past, then we cannot be controlled by pathology. It is only when we look away from that past that we are lost and the dark force of pathology can then control us.

The monster that we project onto the past, that we believe actually exists, becomes a thing that actually does exist. This is why in most dreams, when someone is running after us, it is a good thing because it is usually the Archetypes. But we run anyway. We run until we are most certainly lost from ourselves.

When we become the soul child, we are out of history, out of time. We do not worry about our portfolios, the price of gasoline, how to get money. The whole of history is gone because at the core of it, everything that ever happened was really false.

In fact, in a way, ironically, it never happened. When we are healed and we return to the love, all of it is forgotten. When God forgives, it is all gone. First, we drink of the river of forgetting, and then we drink of the river of remembrance. We remember Him and we remember who we are.

Suddenly, the worry and the external issues are gone. At this moment, we can truly be with the Divine, truly be alien in the flesh. We can be the incarnation of Divine love. It is a gift for everyone – St. John of the Cross pointed the way. The steps in gravity take us down into the valley of the shadow of death.

Every dream takes us a step closer toward and eventually into the valley. This is why things often feel worse before they feel better. It is a tough journey, but it is a journey we can only take with our hearts open. Once taken, we can never go back. There is no back.

It is like the hobbit Frodo in Tolkien's *The Lord of the Rings*. Frodo cannot stay in the Shire after he returns from his journey because he knows something more. What is better than the Shire? Divine love. We all feel bad for Frodo when he leaves the Shire, when he heads off with the elves, when he is going into the process of Dying to Self.

We feel bad for him because we are in the Shire, watching him go away. Our perspective is really from our reluctance to go where he is going. We do not go; instead, we watch him leave into the sunset.

There are no answers for us when we are in the Shire – the answers come only when we take that journey. Every hero walks into the sunset because we cannot know or even conceive of what the hero is walking into.

Stage Three

We Fear What We Have Lost

How many people are willing to stand in their fear and not react? It is the trickiest thing of all because fear invokes fight or flight. We have been trained through tribal generations by lions in the jungle – we get scared and we jump. Our whole physiology is about threat so we associate fear with threat.

But what if fear is not about a threat in the psychological world, in the spiritual world? What if fear is an opportunity to reclaim something lost? We see it as a threat because it is new and unfamiliar. How do we train ourselves to accept fear as an opportunity and not jump away from it but instead jump into it?

To retrain in this way is critical to anyone who journeys through this landscape. Of course, some fears are trauma rooted – but even in these cases, the only solution for trauma is to face into the feeling of it as the dreams guide us.

At first we may feel into the anxiety of the moment. But as we feel into the anxiety, we are simply discovering ourselves in a deeper way as we journey back to our soul. It is remembering who we really are. The anxiety covers up all the ways that we cope, which creates the false self – not just a persona, but a false self that copes with the anxiety.

When we jump away from our fear, we identify with our

false self – the self we create because we do not want to deal with our fear. Reversing that and dropping into the anxiety is the first step of facing into the fear. It is the authentic experience of "I Am That I Am Scared."

But the story does not end there; it continues. The journey deepens into the next layer – which is what is revealed through opening up to the fear. Perhaps in the next dream, the child self will be revealed. What may be revealed is that we are scared of nothingness, a nothingness that does have somethingness.

Remember, in the archetypal journey, we fear what we have lost. Pathology tries to convince us, "No, you are scared because there is nothing there." It is the same thing with dying. We are scared that if we die, we will go into that everlasting sleep where there is zero. But what if it is nothing like that at all? What if it is all about being conscious? We are so trained to believe in nothing that we are scared of peeling back the layer of fear. We are so scared that there is nothing – yet every dream shows us there is more of us than we thought.

The Jacob Factor

Once we feel the presence of the Archetypes, we know the truth. From that moment on, no matter what we do, we are never the same. Even if we run the other way, even if we refuse to face into it.

Once we feel this, we feel what this work can be. Until that moment, it is all in our minds. Our mind can play with dreams and symbols and metaphors and collective unconscious and interpretation forever.

But when we feel it, it is like a lightning bolt crashing through our psyche. Like electrocution. It shatters all of our ignorance for that moment. We might forget, of course. We will. We may never remember again. But in this work, this moment can be the beginning of the end of pathology. Once we feel the presence, it can be the beginning of a new life, if we make the choice to face into it.

Often, when we feel the presence, we may have a follow-up dream that has the potential for the killing of some pathology in us. This does not happen randomly. It does not matter if we are atheist or devoutly religiously – we simply feel it in our bones.

This can open the process of Dying to Self because His

loves provokes us to engage the enemy like nothing else does. This is why the love of the Divine is so initially destructive.

It is like Jacob fighting with the Angel.

One of the steps of this work is that we become like Jacob. We come to a place in ourselves where we fight or we are at war with ourselves. We are at war with pathology; we are not at war with God. It is courageous to be Jacob, no matter how difficult a process, for Jacob never doubted the existence of the Angel.

Once we have a connection with the Divine, even if only for a moment, our illusions are shattered and we feel the truth of that moment, even if we struggle for the rest of our lives to obtain it or to refuse it. That is our choice. We can be Jacob, if we are willing.

If we do not know that feeling, however, if we do not know the presence of that love, we can battle all we want, but we will be like Don Quixote, battling windmills. If we do not know the Divine, then we are just guessing.

Every dream has the potential to show us how we are Jacob struggling with our Angel, within ourselves. We need to be aware of the Jacob factor of our egos. We are not as bad as we think. But we are not as good as we think, either.

We all fight with God. If we think we are not fighting with God, however, we are in the worst shape of all. It is important to acknowledge that fight. We may judge ourselves for fighting, pathology may want to shame us for it, but we are really fighting for our lives.

Jacob is a holy man because he fights for his wholeness. If he did not fight with the Angel, he would be lost.

We all start out lost. We have to realize that our conflict is between God and ourselves, whether we are facing into our traumas, our hurts, or whether we are focused on issues that really do not matter. Perhaps it is the history of our existences, our past lives. No matter what we face, we must have the courage at some point to acknowledge that struggle.

We have to strip off the illusion of how wonderful we are and how terrible somebody else is or how terrible we are – the whole gyroscopic lie. Who cares who is right and who is wrong? The fight is the fight within ourselves.

It is a difficult step. We struggle to reach the place where we are willing to be Jacob, but then we want to be right or wrong, or we want to run. We do not stop and say, "Wow! This is one hell of a fight. Do I really want to be in this?"

Being Jacob is fighting the good fight. We do not have to be perfect. We do not have to figure anything out. This is Jacob's gift. God's gift to Jacob. To commit to where we are – to commit to our struggle, to our fight.

The Complicated Issue of Pain

The issue of pain is a complicated one, like the issue of fear. There are different types of pain just as there are different types of fear – all these feelings are there for different reasons and often have different purposes. Sometimes, the purpose for pain is obvious, that things have happened in our lives that caused pain or caused the soul to have pain.

Then there are things that we have done to others or to ourselves that have caused us pain. We do not necessarily acknowledge this pain, perhaps because it is too painful or we feel too much guilt. But when we get past the guilt, sometimes we are able to know that we are forgiven. We are free to feel our failings or to feel the pain of things we have done to others.

To feel that forgiveness, we must step into our pain and our regret without blame, without judgment.

This allows us to catch up with our own souls. What the soul felt in the past about what happened and what we have done, is what we need to feel. The soul feels all of this, even when we do not. We need to catch up with ourselves by feeling everything our soul has felt.

Catching up with ourselves in the past is saying, "Oh,

this is what I felt when this happened." As we do this, we become more and more congruent with our soul. The places where we feel shame, where we feel entitlement or where we feel justified around things that are not of our soul become barriers to the real authenticity within us.

Does this mean that we go to the people we have hurt and tell them what happened in the past? If we cheated on someone, do we tell our current husband or spouse? These are tough decisions that cannot be answered for anyone. The most important piece is that we need to feel it for ourselves. Acknowledgment of pain allows forgiveness. And even if whatever we did was necessary, if we have soul pain, we need to feel this in order to grow. The mind wants to always say, "I did what was right, why should I feel pain when what I did was justified?"

The soul does not judge. It only feels. The soul feels what is.

When we judge our feelings of pain and go to guilt, this is not of the soul. Guilt is where pathology comes creeping in. Forgiveness is so important because of the guilt – we can stay in the guilt or we can take our pain to the Divine.

Taking that pain to the Divine ensures that we can acknowledge our pain for what it is. It ensures acceptance of ourselves and our own soul's hurt for what has happened. It is through the process of forgiveness and love that takes place when we reveal our pain to the Divine, that the healing of that pain can come. Through this healing, we can come back to our selves.

If we do not allow that process and we feel the pain of our mistakes, we can become trapped in them and fall prey to nihilistic pain. Nihilistic pain is pain without end, where there is no forgiveness and no hope for forgiveness.

The soul always knows forgiveness because forgiveness is part of Divine love. Whatever has happened, it can be felt and it can be forgiven.

Free Will

The free will that is our choice is linked with the passion and capability to understand our own belovedness or our own passion for the belovedness or our own feeling of the Beloved's passion for us.

All of this determines a great deal about our will. Why? Because the more we feel into the love, the more our free will to do the right thing – or the thing that He wants, which is the thing that is in the best interest of our own soul – becomes primary to us. This is not a moral or religious realization but a realization from the heart. When we fail to realize this, we have no free will.

Free will is a manifestation of love. The choices we make from that love strike at the very heart of the existential reality of every single individual on this planet. Somewhere inside of everyone is that love and a choice to either turn away from or to embrace the Beloved, despite what pain has occurred in our lives.

This is such a private moment, and it can change. In one moment, we can turn away from the Beloved for unknown reasons even though the passion is there. The next moment, we may turn back. The unfoldment to the place where the passion and the desire and the choice are fully alive is a process.

To accomplish a deeper revelation of our love for the Divine and the Divine's love for us takes time. It is not a question of making choices, as in doing something our therapist told us to do.

Of course, if we make choices that are not what the Animus wants us to make, it does not necessarily mean that we are bad students. Maybe it is because we have not gotten deep enough in the passion to receive the revelation of the heart.

Being Broken and Being in the Army of the Divine

Pathology is not personal; it is collective. There is a personal level in which we are all engaged with our personal issues and personal way of being with pathology, of course, but pathology exists as one inky black thing that is tentacled to every person. It is real; it has its own kind of soul. It has an embodiment of identity that is not any one person. It is itself, a force to be reckoned with.

In a way, pathology is in battle with the Divine. There is the idea of heaven and hell, good and bad, the devil being at war with God – what this means is unclear, but it is certainly a metaphor for the fact that there is a power struggle. It would be easier to think of it in terms of light and dark, that there is a natural phenomenon of consciousness raising, that we are just ignorant and once we lose our ignorance, we can evolve. It would be much easier to think in this nice way.

But pathology is not just about ignorance. This thing does not want us to evolve. It is a deliberate will that wants to keep us from growing. The dreams clearly reflect that it is not just that we have to learn, but that there is something there that is fighting us tooth and nail. The more we learn, the harder it fights.

When there is an enemy or a war in a dream, the initial layer is that the enemy is our individual pathology. But as we advance in the work, the dreams show that we become soldiers aligned with the Animus. We work for Him, like being in an army, and we are fighting in a war. The war, however, is not just against our own pathology. At some point, our pathology breaks apart and the war becomes against the bigger pathology.

What does this mean? If we reverse the question, then we are on the side of the Divine and the Divine is bigger than the pathology. It is the love in the universe, the physics that holds everything together. The Divine wants to change the world, wants to plant itself here in this plane. The Divine is bigger than big and has everything behind it, everything it wants and needs to do this. The only thing it does not have is the people to embody it.

If the Archetypes can lay claim to our soul and we join their army, then the Divine would come forth. He puts us in this position when we are finally listening to Him; He is finally being heard. We are in His army in this way when a dream shows us we are in, not when we believe that we are.

This is quite tricky. There are those who believe they are in the army because they want to believe it. There are people blowing up other people believing that they are doing it because they are in God's army – Muslims, Catholics, Protestants, Jews. Everywhere we look, there are people like this standing for God.

They cannot all be right and they probably are not right. They are probably all wrong. How many people actually stand with God? How many people in religions stand with God? What if the idea is right but the reality is that no one is actually doing it? What if there is no miracle and we do not know that there is no miracle? What if we do not know that no one is standing with God and we all end up wondering, "Where is God?"

This is tricky because most of the people who believe that they are at the right hand of God are not. But what if we have proof that we standing with God in our dreams? What if we have done a tremendous amount of work and have died to self, and then the dreams show that the Divine steps in? If that is true, miracles can happen.

At the risk of being arrogant, I believe that when we start to get dreams where we are fighting and the Divine is there, then we are living that miracle. If we have gone through years of intense work, if we have gone through the dark night of the soul, when the dreams have validated every step of the journey, then we are ready to live that miracle. And living that miracle may affect the entire world.

The risk is that if we are not totally surrendered, then our egos can go wild. But if we are at the pinnacle, if we are living it as shown by our dreams and not based on what we want to believe, then we are beyond the human condition and part of the spiritual solution.

Again, this is tricky. If we are saying the same thing other people are saying, others who are not living that miracle, who are not in the army of the Divine, then why would anyone believe us?

The truth is that the Divine will use us in the way that is right. Of course, people will read this and say, "I knew you guys were elitists, were cultists. I knew it. You lied to me. This is not therapy at all." The truth is; there are the few who do get cleaned up to the point where the Divine can say, "I want to use you; I want you to be part of my army."

We can know this, not because we think it or want to believe it, but because the dreams show us. Because He comes to us in our dreams in this way that He does not come to others. This is a frightening thing to say but it is important to say it because gravity will eventually, if we let it, truly pull us all the way, take us to the top of the mountain, to the deepest valley.

For those who are truly connected, who have truly done the excruciating work it takes to be connected, there is nothing more terrifying than being the one.

It is not scary to be the megalomaniac who will go up on the cross shouting "Choose me! Choose me!" It is truly terrifying when we are truly with Him. Truly terrifying to step into that abyss, into the archetypal world. It is terrifying even when we have the support, even when we do not have the pride to capture us, because there is no reference point.

There is only an incredible whoosh of wind. It is as if we have gone high enough in the atmosphere to hit the jet stream. This is like the wind we hear, a rushing wind. When we are there, we are part of that energy and flow, not in some fool's eddy down below thinking we are something, thinking we are somewhere.

It is terrifying to be in that wind, that flow. If it is not, then we are not there and our dreams will show it. It is so terrifying because it is so unbelievable. It is beyond what the ego, and the megalomaniac ego, could ever know.

It is terrifying to stand in that whoosh of power and wind, energy and flow, to give ourselves to it and allow it to move us through the world. It is terrifying to stand there in the face of all the projections that will tell us that we are wrong. The dreams will always tell us what is true. If I am wrong, the dreams will show me, too.

The Innate Longing for God

The relationship between the soul self that usually comes in dreams as the child and our ego self can be difficult and ambiguous. There are a variety of issues that this can create. Sometimes the child self carries a wound or the memory of feelings that we have long since lost or denied. The most common way for therapists to address this, including Archetypal Dreamwork therapists, is to point out that this reflects some moment where we lost our child self through trauma or just the process of growing older.

But there is a spiritual issue inherent in the division between the child self and the adult ego self. The child self perceives love not only in terms of its innate vulnerability and need but also in terms of its innate longing for God. For the more spiritually attuned, if not all of us, there is a side to our own life, our spiritual life, that is so pregnant and ripe with feelings of love for God. These feelings are as powerful and strong as love for any human being, even stronger.

It is something innate that comes from a relationship known somewhere, perhaps in other lifetimes, that for whatever reason reflects some kind of profound relationship or knowing of the Divine.

The dreamer's ego, the adult ego that has lost the soul, may feel these feelings from the child self, may feel this energy of Divine love and then mistakenly expect it to be something to claim in the world. We take this energy and look for God in others, thereby constantly feeling wounded because there is no way that anyone could be that Divine Archetypal, Animus being. Even if the other person is nice, is devoted, it just does not work that way. When we look for God in others, we are lost in this world and are perpetually dissatisfied.

If we could reclaim that soul self, then that love and that need could be requited and fulfilled. Then the soul child could be birthed and we could move forward in our spiritual growth. Then, having both the adult self and the child self, we would know and be able to distinguish between emotional feelings with people in the world and Divine feelings.

The natural balance is to not place people in the world in the position of being Divine, or in the position of being irrelevant. In this other extreme, we give up on the whole thing and just have animals or live some kind of reclusive existence. We may say, for example, "I'll just have my cat or my dog – that is all I need." We can go from gushing over every person and getting nothing back to just giving up because of the lack of fulfillment.

When we control a child in a dream, it is our ego controlling our child self. There is no room for the Divine. The Divine is much smarter than we are – any control issues we have just add to the problem. For, with the Animus, we have to surrender control.

It is much "easier" to be with someone in the world who is not going to love us, someone we can blame for everything while we remain in control. Sometimes, we find unrequited love so that we never have to give up control. If we give over to someone so fully and completely, as we would with the Divine, we would have to give up control.

If we want to get close to the Animus, we have to be our soul self. The ego self, even though it may try, cannot have a relationship with the Animus except through a kind of veneer that some people can manage. But the dreams will show if we are having a full relationship with the Animus. This kind of relationship is extremely rare, but it is possible.

Most of us suffer whether we are religious people or spiritual people or not. We suffer the vacuousness of separation. It is our soul we need to die to so we can feel the love from that central aspect of ourselves.

The Primalcy in the Snake's Bite

In a dream, the venom from a snake bite is primalcy. It kills us because the venom/primalcy – the libido or the id, which is on a deeper level of libido – is so toxic to the psyche that once we receive it, we cannot live in our neurotic, shameful self. Shame is the very undoing of primalcy.

In the Divine world or in the Garden of Eden, we knew our innocence, primalcy and passion – we were alive. This is related to the polymorphous perverse state of a child which is simply the fundamental aspect of beingness. Pure being.

There is an aspect of beingness that is essence and a sensitivity to God. Primalcy is something different. The sensitivity is actually imbued with a great energy, a great aliveness, a great power. Primalcy is really the bread and butter of what flows in our veins. It is what allows the penis to be erect. It is what allows a woman's clitoris to stand forth.

Children are very sexual. They achieve some form of orgasm. They have tremendous energy in that way and will often engage with each other sexually. Unfortunately, there are pedophiles who prey on this energy like vultures. One of the worst things that happens to a child who experiences early childhood sexuality is the shame that happens later – it is like leaving heaven all over again. The message is that this thing happened and someone is bad – either the child or the situation or the someone.

It happens when the experience is a rape or molestation but it also happens in children when the experience is with sisters or brothers or friends and the experience was satisfying. These experiences have been called exploratory, but it is really that children are passionate and energized. It is part of who people are. Then they hit the wall of shame later for all the "bad" things they did, which feeds pathology. Shame is its own trigger.

There are so many areas where we lose our innocence. When we lose our innocence and primalcy, the consciousness of primalcy needs to be raised to a spiritual level. Jung talks about the integrity of the psyche and being moral – that it is important when we are older for it is not about running around like a dog. It is really about raising the consciousness of primalcy to a spiritual level.

If our innocence/primalcy is broken on a sexual or sensual level, then all we have for spirituality is essence. Then we are prayerful or devotional but we do not have the primalcy. Often we are dry, boring, moralistic and pedantic and we make God's love boring. It is so important to understand that in the psyche, the primalcy wants to release itself into us.

When the snake bites us in a dream, we are allowing all this primalcy to come back through and to us. It is not that shame dies, it is that we become empowered by the Divine, by this energy that in and of itself awakens us and takes us past our shame. It takes us into this aliveness and the Archetypes can come to us in our dreams to meet us in this newfound aliveness.

So much of what we think we are is more or less a neurotic representation of the self that has been lost. We fashion ourselves without the primalcy. We make ourselves up as a reaction to the world, as a reaction to the loss. It is a reaction to the pain. The self that makes itself up has got to die because the primalcy does not make itself up. It is that it is. "I am that I am." This new self is reflected back in the eyes of the beloved – the Animus and the Anima.

It is not the knowing of God that is forbidden. That is a side-track. The issue is having relationship with the Divine.

If our personal relationship comes from some kind of iconic knowing or knowing from a place of being lost from our real passion, what kind of knowing is it anyway? What kind of experience is it anyway? But if we are in our passion and our essence and our energy, then the Animus – particularly with women – can come in a conjunctio manner, in a sexual manner. He enters us. This wakens the child to the clitoris. All of this is driven through the primalcy.

Everybody is capable of relationship of some sort. But when we explore the "I" relationship, we are talking about only that which can only be understood when we uncover the full passion. The relationship is manifested in a greater knowing of that passion – that knowing of the Divine through the emergence of the self that is passionate. Then there is a knowing of the Divine in a profound way.

Prometheus represents this knowing as the fire giver – the fire is the passion. That kind of enlightenment is so uniquely personal and unknowable – the mind cannot know this. It is conjecture. Many people may believe they have relationship with the Animus, but to have it through the primalcy, through the whole cauldron of the dream process, to be in that soup of the energy that the dreams work within us until it is released, is really what this work is all about.

It is not the knowing of the mind knowing God, it is about the energy and the passion of that life force that becomes part of the conscious experience of the Divine.

That relationship is completely different – this is why relationship is a loaded word. We could all say "being in relationship with Him," and everyone would know what we were talking about because everyone understands that word. But most of us do not understand relationship through primalcy. We do not understand relationship through conjunctio and the release of that orgasmic self of the child. That is not understood. It is forgotten and lost. It fell back into the unconscious long before a person was even eight or nine years old.

Most of us hate our primalcy or we hate the vulnerability or the passion or the pain or the creativity. There is always something about it we hate.

We all also have some primalcy we adhere to, something that gives us emotion or feeling whether it is sexuality, pain, anger, nihilism. But if it is not everything it can be that has the pure seed of the snake's venom, then we do not have it. The only one that knows what it really is besides the Archetypes is our Divine child self.

And that child self comes through dreams. We might think we know what this is because our mind is very good at thinking things about things. Therein lies the bigger lie. The truth comes in our dreams.

Primalcy is the very essence of the ability to live in our lives with the sense of our own identity and the directedness and potency that allows us to feel and experience the world in terms of our own soul. Primalcy is the thing that should wake us up in the morning.

It is how the Animus can enter us and how we feel that power in ourselves. We can then have these feelings of ecstatic presence and excitement and energy and aliveness, which are all aspects of love.

When we repress such radioactive material as this, we can become extremely sick. We can become nihilistic or compulsive or jealous or competitive or depressed or even suicidal. Often we will have addictive behaviors because when this energy is blocked, it kicks back at us. The energy cannot be adequately repressed so it comes out in some other way that is not healthy for us.

We suffer because the very thing that would empower us, disempowers us. It turns into something Freud called thanatos, a destructive desire to die. Something that is actually killing us has its genesis as something wonderful.

Letting the Primalcy Take Over

The primal self does not fit into society. The primal self sees the lie playing in the world and hates it. Every generation embodies this energy by rebelling against the previous generation.

We have all rebelled. What is the rebellion? The rebellion is the rage against the machine. One moment we are raging against the machine and then we *are* the machine and the next generation is raging against us.

We all become a part of the pathology. We all grow into adulthood and become the very thing we hated in our parents – although most of us do not have the courage to admit it. Our parents were wrong but we are right and now our children are wrong.

On some level, every adolescent child sees the lie of society. There is nothing a parent can do about it. We have to be parents, we have to help our children adapt to the world, otherwise we are doing them a disservice. But still, we are supporting an insanity. We do not have any choice as parents.

The bottom line is that the primalcy in all of us wants to say, "I'm tired of it!" That primalcy is in jail all over the world. It is imprisoned in our souls and it acts out in ways that allow the pathology to destroy its very intention. Our rules preclude the acting out part, but the intention of acting out is to wake us up! It is connected to the soul, it is connected to God in some way and it is saying, "Enough already!"

The world does not like this part.

Often the primalcy is underneath the trauma and we cannot get to the primalcy without cutting through the trauma and all the ways we manage it. The reason we are traumatized is that we have repressed our primalcy.

If we were in the truth of ourselves, we would be free to live our primalcy, letting it be part of the evolution of our souls. If we could grow from that place, we would not have to go through trauma to grow. But instead, the raw material of our souls lies under the trauma.

When we first encounter the primalcy, anger and rage, it may come in the moment when it feels like we are disconnected from the Animus. We may believe that our primalcy is inherently disconnected from the Divine. Instead, we are in opposition to the primalcy and it is not the time to look for the Animus. This is the time to let that primalcy take us over.

That primalcy is in fact an extension of the love that the Animus has for us. We always look at the Animus and the Archetypes for a relationship, which is great, but when we are Dying to Self, we are becoming something new.

At this moment, it is not the time for the Animus to come and rescue us. It is the time for us to go through our trauma alone knowing the love is there. The love is resurrecting the soul that was lost. This is a very painful process. The Animus is not leaving us – we simply have to learn to be ourselves.

Sometimes we can use the Animus to avoid finding ourselves because we have Him already. But it does not work that way. We have to not only learn to be in relationship with the Divine but also we have to be willing to become what we lost. We have to become the self that was lost and then continue to grow and evolve. It is not just about relationship; it is about becoming who we are.

Our relationship with the Animus is never going to be compromised by discovering our primalcy. It is not true. It is just a different kind of work.

We have to die and lose ourselves, but it does not mean we have lost Him. Wanting to just be close to the Animus so that everything will be fine is more like religiosity. Yes, we need to be with the Animus, but we also have to go through our own transformational experience.

The goal of the work is not just to be with the Divine, but also to die to self. The Archetypes do not want us just to be dependent on them. The Archetypes want us to become the Divine inspiration of the glint in God's eye that created us in the first place.

When Fear Covers Hurt

When fear covers hurt, there is no gateway through fear except through pain. In this case, fear is a layer with hurt underneath it.

Fear's job is often to open the door to other feelings. It can be to the unknown; it can be to our passion. When the door opens to pain, this usually reflects trauma that has been repressed. When we are traumatized, we are scared and we get hurt, creating layering.

When we work through trauma and we do not have fear covering for another feeling, then fear can become its own alchemical portal. It can transmute into God consciousness or into essence, as discussed in an earlier essay.

But when fear transfers into a kind of hysteria, we become frenetic in some way – compulsively cleaning or eating, doing good in the world, working, gambling – it can be anything. Underneath the compulsiveness, fear becomes something else – shame or responsibility or depression. They all have the same root.

We want to believe that if we function, and especially if we function well, then we are not depressed. This is not true. When we are Renaissance, which means we can do everything and do it well, we may be very high functioning, but we may be more depressed than someone who is not functioning. No one would ever know when we are so successful – no one would ever know how much we really suffer.

Renaissance people who do well do not want to be seen. If seen, then the "successful" personas are at risk. In this case, fear that hides pain will mutate into shame.

There can be multiple layers – the alchemical fear can be so deep that we have shame, fear, pain then fear again. When fear reappears after we have worked through the shame, fear and pain, then it can revert to Archetypal fear. The psyche can move into relationship with something more powerful.

To know the Animus through this kind of fear is a deeper transformation or a deeper surrender. This is why we are afraid at this layer. In Alchemy, we always feel fear because the psyche breaks down again. But when the psyche breaks down in this place, under all the layers, it is not to a place of nomenclature referencing trauma, but rather a new nomenclature that references enlightenment and the true gifts of the spirit. The true gift of fear is that it is a feeling corridor that alchemizes into essence and enlightenment and connection to the Divine self.

The release for fear, in this case, is always the same – pain. Once we feel the pain, then the top layer of fear is gone. Then we can move through the pain and get to the deeper, alchemical fear.

When the pain is repressed, we do not get to have our pain about anything because it all gets related to the trauma. But when we go deep enough and the fear arises, the opportunities for spiritual growth can emerge. The pain is still there – it becomes the rudimentary beginning for compassion and our own beingness. In other words, we feel things from ourselves, which is new. When we repress our pain and have trauma around our pain, any pain we may feel will usually be for someone else.

But when the pain is accepted and fear goes to pain, it is simply normal pain, part of a heart that reflects pain, joy, grief, any feeling. It is no longer an issue about the trauma of pain. We feel pain because of what happened, and now it can become just the pain of the moment. Our pain.

When we work through our trauma pain and go into our real feelings – our fear, our pain – our real hearts emerge. We can then truly care for others, but always in relationship to our own sense of loss. It does not come from pity. Instead, when we feel our own sense of loss, we have compassion.

❊ ❊ ❊ ❊

A big question in the unfoldment process, in spiritual enlightenment, is what happens when fear no longer hides a feeling or opens a door to something else. What does fear do then? When fear is released in this way, it can return to its normal state.

Fear is a mutation of not knowing. We naturally are souls who know the Divine and have the capacity to feel Him all the time. This is our natural state of being. When we lose that connection to our soul, our child self, and then to the Divine, we become fearful. It is like being a little child and suddenly not knowing where your father is or where you are.

We can manage this, creating a personality that fits in. But like that child, we have all lost our way. This is where the Alchemy fear is.

This fear will become an intuitiveness, an ability to know the Divine. We would know what He wants us to say or how He would have us manifest – which is the same thing that we want. This is about being who we truly are. When we know who we are as who the Divine created, we are always reflecting ourselves and the Divine.

When we know our pain can take us to our fear, we can get to that underlying experience of love. If we do not know the pain, we can never feel the love. When we do not know the pain, it becomes locked up through fear and then under shame. But we can receive the love by standing in our fear of the Divine. Standing naked in front of the Divine.

THE EVOLUTION OF THE CHILD SELF

One of the most difficult issues is the child self. In general, the girl has been seen as representing the ability to receive and some kind of feeling or capacity for relationship with other, intimacy, while the boy has represented desires or libido or selfness. While this is true, it is only really a shortcut, for it is just touching on a label.

But when we go deeper in our work, the child becomes about more advanced work. The dreams have shown us more about the role of the soul self and the incredibly miraculous way in which the child self is part of the unfolding of consciousness.

There are two stages of child development in dreams. The first is when we encounter a child in a dream that is separate from us. In this situation, we may love the child, we may hate the child, we may want to take care of the child, we may want to be the parent, we may even want to hurt the child.

The child may be healthy, may be injured, may be in a dumpster, may even be dead. It is to our advantage if the child is healthy, but however the child appears, it is always important. In this stage, the core issue is about accepting the child.

Once we have accepted the child, the second stage of development is becoming the child. Becoming the child means that there must be a death of the self. We cannot be the child and be who we have become. We have to die. Many of us have a hard time with this work because although we may like the child, we may like to nurture the child, or we may even feel childlike at times, it is really just ego self-soothing.

But what happens when we get beyond becoming the child? There are two children in all of us, one male and one female, and they typically work together just as the Anima and the Animus work together. The difference, however, is that we are the two things, and as they evolve in us, we become different, more conscious, more aware of things.

The child is so fragile, both the boy and the girl, that not only can it not inhabit us if we are in reaction, but it also cannot evolve. When we move beyond reactions, when we move beyond projecting our pain out, when we have gone through our trauma and come out the other side, we begin to experience the three rungs of Jacob's Ladder – essence, sensuality and grace.

Once this begins to happen, then the boy and the girl can begin to involve themselves in the psyche. The evolution of consciousness is the evolution of the soul, and the child self is the soul self.

The soul can actually begin to participate in the work. It is extraordinary because the boy and the girl are usually very passive functionaries in dreams. But as people in this work are advancing to transcendence that is beyond reaction, beyond trauma, the children are actually having a part. They reveal a deeper mystery.

Most of our stories talk about reaching the end of a journey and then the hero or heroine of the story heads off into something new and unknown. Frodo in *The Lord of the Rings* trilogy cannot fit back into society after his journey to destroy the ring. Instead, he is invited to sail to the West with the immortal elves. In the *Matrix* movie trilogy, after everything is over, the last scene is of a sunrise and the movement into day.

But this is where the stories end. No one really knows this other reality because human beings are not moving beyond the transcendence.

Transcendence is all an idea, and we seek that relationship with God, but working with dreams in this way can help us move through transcendence and actually explore regions of the psyche that I do not believe have been experienced by many people. It seems that some who have written have reached this place, certain saints or poets like Rumi, but it is impossible to really know if they reached it.

Transcendence is felt initially as a disassociation from reality because essence and sensuality and grace are kind of a psychotic realm. What fills the vacuum, however, are the boy and the girl and their extraordinary awareness – that which was so wounded, so vulnerable, that which we would not want to be a part of again.

Trauma vulnerability leads to trauma, which leads to more vulnerability – this is a way to become open to the Divine. But, beyond that, to realize that the soul itself is vulnerable as it is in the world is an extraordinarily developed inner life.

When the soul comes into the world, it gets splintered and destroyed.

In its natural home, heaven, as some call it, the soul is powerful and vulnerable and open and potent. To bring that consciousness into this plane through the boy and the girl is what the psyche seems to want to do, as if it is the hidden agenda.

Third Stage dreamwork has been seen as the calling, the way in which we manifest the relationship with the Divine into the world. It is also a deeper psychospiritual journey with a great deal more inner development.

This does manifest in the world, of course. The world is no longer an obstruction because everything we do in the outer world is connected to the inner world. The child has free reign to grow to be what it really was all along. There are no encumbrances in heaven; there are only encumbrances here.

When the child is free of the encumbrances here, which are the ways that our egos survive, then it is free to truly, completely manifest itself. It does this in relationship to its other half. The boy and the girl work in tandem, bringing the androgynous or the hermaphroditic culmination. The child is transgender insofar as in bringing together those elements our consciousness produces the female and male principles.

The other creates the other, just as when we take a male or female hormone. The result is that it triggers a reaction where the other is created: in taking testosterone, estrogen is produced. In the same way, the boy and the girl really create each other. To be the girl, we need the boy, and to be the boy, we need the girl. Each is interdependent on the other.

If we have a psychological abruption where we have a problem in one of the gender identifications within the self, then this must be corrected for the other child to emerge. The boy and the girl both depend on us being able to accept this. Of course, our hormones and social issues also figure into this issue.

At a deeper level, there are issues that the child self will work out because, ultimately, the boy and the girl are the one child. The soul is one gender, with both a penis and a vagina. Men become vaginal. Once they develop enough with the Father, once they are grounded in the male enough, they can reverse it and become women in the sense of being open to God in a vaginal sense.

It is the same with women in reverse. Becoming the girl, becoming grounded in the girl, they become Valkyries with the sword, the sword that is a penis. The Valkyrie is not a Renaissance woman, but a woman who can be a man because she has plumbed the depths of her feminine side with the Animus, because she has entered into conjunctio.

Most women, when they grow into womanhood, lose their vulnerability, lose the girl part of themselves. When they become women without the girl, there is no Anima, for the Anima is always the girl and the woman at the same time. The Animus is always the boy and the girl at the same time.

When we dream, we often see only the aspect of the male or the female that needs to be resolved in the moment as presented by a dream. But, looking at the full range of the male and the full range of the female, it is the whole range from infancy to old age. It is the son, the daughter, the father, the mother, adolescence, prepuberty, adulthood, old age – for both men and women. It is all of these aspects, all in one.

When a woman loses her little girl and her vulnerability to become a woman without that girl, she becomes a high-coping Renaissance woman or a woman who is constantly immature. The women who are constantly immature are the girls who never become women.

It is the same with men; there are those who become men without the boy or who become men as the boy without the true male principle. There is always some combination of not being the whole of ourselves, the whole woman or the whole man. When we do this, we stay identified with whatever part of the developmental process we are in. If we are sixty-five, then we are crotchety or opinionated, but we are not the boy or the girl. The point is to be everything, to be all of these things in every moment.

A man has to return to the male to become a girl. A woman has to truly find her femaleness to then become the boy. This continues to move back and forth, continuing. The man who becomes the girl will eventually come back to the boy, and the woman who becomes the boy will eventually come back to the girl. In the return is a new evolution of understanding of the female and male principles so that the boy and the girl can continue to help us evolve.

Dark Matter

What is love? I challenge our perception of that word. The better question is: What is vulnerability? We cannot fully feel or receive love if we do not know vulnerability.

When we are vulnerable, we know. "I do not need to do anything to be loved." When we are not vulnerable, we can turn this around: "I need to do something to get love." When we say this, we are really saying, "I need to do something to avoid my vulnerability, to avoid the love that would come to me in my vulnerability."

Being loved is excruciating. It is scary. We would rather be accepted and acknowledged for what we have done than be turned inside out. We would rather be loved for the outside.

But the vulnerable child does not say, "Love me because I mowed the lawn." The child, at three, at seven, at eight, just wants to be loved and to be loved without condition. There is nothing a child can give us.

When we begin to realize as children that we are not going to be loved unless we give our parents something, we immediately start to lose our own identity.

We become neurotic, and then the child self is gone. The child can only maintain the child self to the extent that he or she is vulnerable and loved completely without condition.

What this means for us as adults is the complete and utter emasculation of how we have coped, survived and engaged in the world. When we take that away, we no longer know how to relate or engage in the world. We must learn who we are in this new way.

The world is actually so toxic, generally speaking, and it wants to gobble up everything that is precious and vulnerable. Most of us are agents of this in some unintended way because of our disconnection from ourselves. This is not because we want to hurt ourselves or others. It is because we are disconnected from our vulnerability.

When we become open and vulnerable through our work, we invite projections. So, when we become open, we must also become potent. The potency that comes through the vulnerability allows us to be in the world in an authentic way. But when we start to do this level of the work, we actually feel totally powerless. When we feel this, we may also fear the fear of being gobbled up ourselves or of being hurt or wounded, because this probably happened somewhere in our past.

We often confuse control and power with potency. Potency is the capability to develop ourselves through Divine love and the connectedness to our souls. It is a certainty of self that is grounded in the love, in the Divine passion.

Once we give ourselves to that energy unflinchingly, we fulfill our calling and can serve God from that place. This is primalcy.

Freud called this libido. Maybe the deeper aspect of libido that Freud referred to as id is, from my perspective, the will of God. When the libido is aligned with God through the soul, then the energy just surges and fumes through us.

Having this connection with the Divine empowers and imbues us from within, from the soul self. It is through that deepest place that we can manifest our beingness into the world. When we try to manifest the other way around, the world triggers us to react and respond in such a way that we are constantly trying to develop an identity with the world.

Primalcy has nothing to do with this kind of identity with the world. It is the power that exists in the universe coming through us – through our own particular beingness, which is the soul.

This kind of potency is very experiential. To find it, we have to go through the arduous journey of Dying to Self, reclaiming that which is beyond this world, beyond our memories and beyond our experiences. It has nothing to do with our experiences. It has to do with what flows underneath all our ego driven mechanisms – and it is always there.

There is a dream image that reflects this. The dreamer is in her house and there is either an opening in the floor through which she sees a river flowing underneath the house or there is a little door that goes to the river. This kind of dream shows that the dreamer is living in the house while there is an entirely different energy underneath that is completely unrelated.

The river, in a sense, is trying to undermine the house, which is the nature of water. Eventually, the dreams change to where the water actually breaks down the foundation and floods into the first floor. It is wanting the dreamer to be in the river, flowing down the river along with the current rather than being in the house. The current is again a reflection of gravity, of the energy and the pull of the universe.

Scientists have recently discovered dark matter in the universe, and, through this discovery, have realized that the universe is doing an extraordinary thing we did not realize.

We believed that, after the big bang, all the planets would move continually out until losing their impetus and momentum. Eventually, we postulated, they would all fall back upon themselves. For after 15 billion years, according to our understanding of physics, the thrust of the explosion would be over.

This is not what is happening. The universe is actually expanding and picking up speed. The speed of movement is much faster than what should be happening.

Scientists believe that dark matter, whatever it is, is causing the deeper physics of the expanding universe. The cannot see dark matter, but they can track it by phenomena that happen around it. This shows that there are other currents underneath the universe as we know it.

In this work, the water under the building, the unseen soul, the will of the Divine, the Archetypal Reality that we do not see is the dark matter.

Why is pathology not the dark matter? Because everything we see as truth and light through the eyes of our ego is really more or less pathology. Pathology exists on the surface of things, in the physical reality. It does not exist underneath. Just as the slowing of the universe is an illusion, so is the idea that pathology's reality is true. It is all false.

Just as the science of the expanding universe is not valid, so the science of the psyche is not valid. The science of this reality is not valid. As we come to the apocalyptic time, we are discovering that everything we ever thought about anything is wrong.

There is something else controlling things, and we have no idea what it is. To discover this through science is to come full circle back to the Gnostics, the sages, the mystics. The split between science and the spiritual is no longer a split. The scientists are seeing into the physical universe and finding the same underlying truth. They may not call it God, but it is the same underlying something that the sages have talked about since people first felt or were visited by Divine reality.

We have struggled with the issue of letting how we survive in the world, the personalities that we develop out of that world die to the dark matter which is the soul.

The soul self has an entirely different consciousness, an entirely different will, an entirely different reason for being than our personalities. If we could be that child, soul self for an instant, be fully in its potency and knowledge, we would realize that its intelligence is beyond anything we have ever dreamed.

When we do this work and begin to grow into the soul self, we become enlightened by seeing and understanding things that cannot be known by reading. We have to die to this way of understanding, this way of knowing, as it unfolds in us like the petals of a flower. Like the very explosion of the universe, constantly getting stronger and bigger, our consciousness has the same potential. We have the potential of knowing things in a wider perspective than just our petty little survival selves.

When we move into the triangulation of Alchemy, this dark matter, this gravity, begins the job of dissolving the old self. We become more vulnerable and open to the energy of that gravity, of the primalcy, of our own beingness.

It is the vulnerability that opens us to this deeper mystery.

The Soul's Song

There are those of us who want to serve God, but when put to the task of doing the intensive work through the dreams, we are rarely given the gift. It requires a tremendous commitment of evolutionary proportions to be fully given the gift of His guidance in a direct and immediate way.

When we are given it, we know it. We know it in our dreams and in our lives. It is a powerful fiat in our hearts – a call to action of some sort. But only with the fires of devotion, only through the opening of the soul and the deepest level of self can this be. Without the soul, our desires often reflect or come from somewhere else – will, guilt, commitment, obligation, duty. The soul, on the other hand, only wants to be near Him.

The "orders" are only an expression of His love for us when we are in our souls. They are not orders. To have such awareness and sensitivity is to be connected to one's child self.

That is the work, the opening of that self.

But many of us would rather say, "Give me the orders, already. Just tell me what to do!" His response is to wait until we have become the fruit of His love, until we awaken to the child self, to the soul. He waits for us to ripen like fruit.

The soul's song is the perfect balance between passion

and devotion. Passion without devotion can be creativity, but without the spiritual connection. Many believe that being close to God is a sacred, quiet thing. Quiet is good, but passion is noisy. It is loud. It often appears boisterous and even aggressive. But when passion is directed toward Him and the expression of it is part of the devotion for Him, then it can be an expression of devotion – even it is a form of anger.

Devotion is intertwined with need. When we are obedient, relating to dutiful aspects, we are not in our need. We are tied up with being good, with performing, with fulfilling a mandate. The need for His love is the root of all devotion. When we need Him in this way, there is no fear.

Fear cannot exist when we are devoted to Him because when we are devoted, we know He never dies. Even if we die, we are with Him. We have fear when we do not know Him or are not deep enough in our devotion to know Him.

Quietude and sacredness are not distinctly separate from noise and aggression as part of an expression of the energy of devotion – of leaping from building to building or shouting for joy, for example. There are all aspects of sacredness and potency. Pathology likes us to be quiet only. It likes to say, "Shush, be quiet, behave this way. Fold your hands that way. Pray like this. Meditate like that. Hush." Sometimes prayer life is noisy, sometimes it is chaotic, aggressive and energetic. It is never without heat and heart.

And, it is unique in the world. The soul cannot be faked, cannot be mitigated by structures or conformity to rituals when it abounds and is free. It must be allowed to be free like a child running on the beach, running with horses, the surf pounding and the wind roaring.

The Question of God

The question of God is really what God means to each individual because God is unique to each and every one of us. This experience of each person is the only important experience of the Divine because it is about our relationship as well as who we are in terms of that relationship.

In an abstract, esoteric understanding of God, there is no place for us, no place for the individual. Dreams are so great because the Archetype in the dreams is always wanting intimacy with us – an intimacy that is unique and specific to each of us.

In this experience, God is not an abstract idea; God is an actual, unique, personal experience of love, direction, belongingness. This is the only real knowing that is worth knowing. When we try to relate to God as a concept and as a belief, then God is just a word. But when we encounter some aspect of the Divine in our dream life or even in our outer life, then our question of God is answered because we are having a particular experience that does not ask the questions of how or what or why.

It is simply an experience. The experience is much more intimate. These encounters, which happen when we get deep enough in our work, usually happen more often in our dream life because we are more open to the Divine in our unconscious when we are asleep.

When we do have these encounters, then this is what we live for – the next, deeper experience of the Divine in the next deeper dream or experience. We can drink from these experiences, even get drunk from them. In this state, we find that we do not care about the other questions because they are all intellectual.

There is no feeling to a concept of God as the creator of all things. There is a feeling, however, in a dream when we are having an experience with the Divine, such as jumping into the Archetype's arms.

In our encounter with the Divine in our dreams, we have feelings such as joy, pleasure, love, sadness, grief.

Having our own experience and feelings and relationship with the Divine is far more satisfying than the concept of God as the great creator of all things. If we stay with this concept, then the ego can create ideas about how to be with God, such as being good. This is a dry and tyrannical way of thinking. This is not what God wants. God wants to be in relationship with us.

The Lie of the Apocalypse

What is the Apocalypse? What does the Apocalypse have to do with the death of self? What does the death of self have to do with annihilation? What does annihilation have to do with death? Big words. Complicated issues. Subject matter often perceived as irrelevant.

Irrelevant... or is it merely a play on a reality that has been overlooked?

Fundamentally, Apocalypse means the end of the world. Annihilation means the destruction of everything we know. But what is death of self? We do not know what that means, but every night's sleep ultimately invites us to find out. Every night's of sleep would have us come closer to actually Dying to Self.

The idea of Dying to Self awakens within us the idea of genesis or the birth of something new, a sense of transcendence that we can sense only as a vague urge, a nuance, a perception. We dance on the top of a pin, our minds spinning around trying to understand how things are. We do not understand how things are; we do not have knowledge of reality.

What is past death, past annihilation, is everlasting life. If we die to self, we have everlasting life, life-everlasting.

Words that play on words. Concepts that bridge other ideas together.

All the teachers talk of a place. The job of dreams is to break the veil so we can find the place where we can live in harmony with the Divine self. Live as a god with gods, live the Divine within us with the Divine; that which is of God, goes back to God.

But all this is after we die? Or could this death be something that can happen in life? The Apocalypse happens in life; it is about our current situation in this dimension; it is about the world as we know it. It is not about something later on; it is now. In the physicalness of reality, in the physicalness of our body, the Apocalypse is about the death of self – now.

The four horsemen of the Apocalypse lead us to the descent of spirit into matter, the alchemical process in which two becomes three becomes four becomes two. The four is the four horsemen of the Apocalypse; the four is the point of death. The four becomes two. Two, in the final analysis, is after the Apocalypse, after the four horsemen, after Alchemy has done its job.

The movement into an alchemical reality is the Apocalypse. If we wait around for the end of the world, we are only talking about the end of ourselves and the beginning of a true self. We wait for the end of the world not realizing it is us that has to die to become born.

The end of the world is an idea that comes from pathology. The Apocalypse itself is nothing more than a little man who lies to us, a little man who takes our own personal death and twists it to distraction. All our hopes for the new world, for a new life, are dashed. We look down the black hole, the deep well, and see the end of the world.

We keep looking in and seeing nothing but death: A meteorite crashing into the earth. Ecosystems dying. Apocalypse is death. The world cannot sustain itself. We cannot breathe the air; it is on fire. The Apocalypse, the conflagration, the great end…

What if all of this is fear projected from the place where we personally must find our demise.

What if the Apocalypse is a lie meant to distract us from the true purpose of the four horsemen – the Alchemy of self, the death of self. What if there is no Apocalypse except one's own personal Apocalypse? What if the world continues?

There is no end of the world. The resurrection is really the ascent of all souls, is the expression of our Divine selves finding the love of God.

Why must this life be anything more than that? Because the little pathological man, Mr. Apocalypse, wants it to be more. This is the big lie, the big ruse that it is all outside of ourselves. What has to die is out there; therefore, the world must die. Another lie.

Do not be afraid, for the death is the death we need to move through in order to find ourselves on this plane, in this life. This is what we are doing. It is not the end of anything. It is learning the ability to transcend and become part of Divine consciousness. It is not something to be feared. It is something to be welcomed.

Fear is the lie that makes us run from our dreams, makes us run from our psyches. It is the lie through which we see the psyche as nothing more than pieces of a puzzle that have no meaning except as a reflection of a greater struggle within the outer world.

But there is no struggle in the outer world. The struggle is inside every one of us – to deny or find the truth, to become conscious, to die to self.

But what if the failure of the collective whole to do such a thing creates an Apocalypse in the world in which the world must die because we individually will not? Is then the Apocalypse real? Is the end of the world imminent, if we do not die to self? Our minds latch on, feed on hate, retribution, failure, thanatos, nihilism. This idea that the world comes to an end because we fail to find the Divine is yet another lie from Mr. Apocalypse. For we cannot fail. There cannot be an ending. It is destiny.

We must and can find the way through. The lie is that we will not. The fear is that something will happen outside of us. It is all projection. The greatest fear is what we are afraid of within us. It is what we can become, what is possible for all of us.

It is the fear of children who forgot themselves, who never really grew up. It is a psychotic lie marbled through humanity's collective psyche. We live in fear. We die in fear. Or we live in an illusion of love and power that does not exist in our consciousness at the moment. There is a way through.

Every night the psyche knocks on our door. The Divine comes through, saying, "Follow this path. Come this way." We do not have to guess if and what our lives could become. It is there every night calling to us – the third of the brain not used, the third of the life not lived, the promise, the door, the portal in which we find ourselves anew. In the gap, in the vacuum of such a thing, the lie is created, the fear is projected. And the nightmare is hatched.

The Baby as Our Divine Spark

The child self, the polymorphous perverse self, is the vulnerable soul self in dreams. But what about when a baby appears in a dream? We often construe the baby as a younger version of the soul, so that as the soul comes into life, the baby dies early. But there may be another meaning.

The baby in a dream does not really grow up, not in the eternal sense. The motif of the baby is really the eternal, hoped-for self. When a baby is being born or is healthy in a dream, it is some potential self within us that, as it grows, manifests. But once it grows, it is no longer a baby. It becomes something else. In this way, the baby is the precursor to the child. Growing older from a baby to a child, it remains always autonomous to its meaning.

The baby, then, is always the potential of what God planned, the spark of what God gave each of us to do. It is the Divine spark and it is an arcane moment of possibility – which is different from the child soul.

The baby is always the potential manifestation for something new. If a baby dies or is dead in a dream, it could be that every time the moment reemerges for the manifestation of something new, the fear related to that baby also reemerges

– almost as a passage. Can this be healed? Perhaps it can be healed, or perhaps it is perpetually a passage for that person every time something new comes into being. This distinction is specific to the individual.

Does the baby that has died actually need to become alive and grow and be healed? Yes. But every time there is something new in that person's spiritual life – something in terms of the potential that was always present – then, maybe the terror and fear of the baby's moment just reappears over and over again. Something happened as a child that the baby could not know. The potential, the baby, did not have a vehicle for it.

On the other side of the equation is life's abundant potential to allow that new spark of something to manifest in one's life. In the case of the dead baby, perhaps when the dreamer comes to the point of the potential being born, it is almost like going back through the passage of fear and pain, all over again.

But rather than seeing this as some terrible loss, it is really an indicator of a great gain. The emergence of something new resupposes revisiting the moment of that loss, the moment the baby died. The potential, however, is not about the loss. The potential is about some transcendent growth.

There are not many people with dreams of babies who have died. The challenge for this kind of situation is to manifest in the moment when the fear exists. I also believe that the loss of children or even the death of a child in a dream is the same potential. We have to grow past this passage.

The death of an older child in a dream usually shows that something traumatic happened and may suggest that in another life, the dreamer died at that age. The baby is more of an innocent and presupposes a greater potential of spiritual possibility because it is a baby.

When there is a trauma of a dead baby, it is not something that is grounded in the potentiality of babies, that the baby will come back to life. This kind of trauma is also not grounded in the world as such because we are not developed enough as babies to have a worldly issue in the first place.

For example, one dreamer has the recurring image of a dead baby in a dream every time something emerges in her spiritual life. The image and the fear in the dream around the image appear as an opportunity to rebirth the child in this situation. Rather than a cause for alarm, it is a cause for celebration. In time, a new spiritual part of her will manifest, for the baby's potential is always spiritual rather than psychological or emotional.

All change, all evolution, spikes around a moment of fear. For this dreamer, the fear comes every time new spiritual consciousness or the opportunity for emergence occurs.

Again, to reiterate, it would be a greater concern if this dead child in the dream were an older child. Then, there would be a trauma wound around that age. In that sense, the baby is less of a concern in terms of trauma in this way.

The world does not want the baby, anyway. The world never wants the baby. Christmas is about the baby, and the Christ child symbolized by the celebration is often left out of the picture. In the movie 2001, A Space Odyssey, the final image is the child in an embryonic state because it is the most powerful image. The child in this state is the potential.

The world needs this child. The world needs anything that relates to such an emergence. Enlightenment passes through that as an image.

Yet, emergence is completely rejected by the world. This is an extremely esoteric point: the pathological illness, this alien virus that has deranged our senses and our hearts, does not allow for the baby to exist in this world.

If we took all of our traumas and put them all together, they do not even begin to reflect the greater trauma of how pathology has successfully kept that Divine child spark away from all of us. We experience it on an emotional, personal level, but in a grander sense, this is a problem of all humankind. All of us can point to a personal trauma that reflects a personal hurt. But even without trauma, the child has been kept from all of us.

The issue is: Are we the child who has trauma from parents or circumstances, or are we connected to the baby that was never born? Regardless of any rejection we have experienced, the baby would still never be born because it was never born on the planet to begin with. We all carry the pain of this awareness.

Do we look at our own personal traumas? Yes, but when we have worked through them, the pain is there anyway. On a collective level, the human suffering and the human wound is what we understand and feel – including the associated fear. We confuse the wound of trauma with the spiritual wound if we are fortunate enough to have a spiritual wound.

I believe that a baby dying in a dream shows a spiritual wound. Another spiritual wound may manifest in a dream as a stigmata image – perhaps blood coming out of palms or feet. In a way, the death of the baby is also a kind of stigmata. If we have these kinds of dreams, we suffer for the disease that has destroyed humankind.

Carrying that wound and understanding the associative fear and pain is in the larger arc of human suffering. But, when we take something archetypal, such as this, and bring it into the personal realm, especially when it does not belong in the personal realm, it amplifies the personal in a negative and destructive way. It almost inflates the personal trauma to a level of absurdity; throwing spiritual suffering into the personal only advances the cause of pathology. But when we take the spiritual suffering out of the personal realm, we can shift the pain and fear so that they are less destructive.

Perhaps when the collective suffering enhances the personal trauma in this way, when it flips the wrong way, it feels as if it is almost impossible to heal.

Standing Where the Dreams Speak

Working with Others

When we are not in the place where the light is coming through, we are not in the openness where God, truth, love and light can come into us. When we work with others as a dreamwork therapist, we stand in the place where the light comes through, the place that is just a crack.

We are always a stone's throw away from connecting the outer world and the inner world; the dream is the doorway. Our dream opens us up, even in just the telling of the dream to someone else. It is sacred. And it is radioactive. If we simple behold the dream, reference it, talk about it, feel into it rather than projecting it, pontificating about it, making ideas about it, then we can feel the intention of it. When we feel the intention of the dream, we do not rob it of its feeling or intention by superimposing our own pathology or intellectualization onto it.

If we can find the place where we stand with God, then the dream will speak to us. As dreamwork therapists, we know that if we are not standing in that openness with God within ourselves, if we cannot hear Him for ourselves, then how could we understand what God is saying to someone else?

Just talking about a dream is so powerful because it

forces us away from ourselves. The dream presents the sane reality, the only truth that is speaking to us or to someone we are working with in the moment. When we stand in the truth as a therapist and when the dreamer stands in the truth, then there is clarity. The dreamer can feel, maybe for the first time since childhood, something that is true by simply acknowledging something in a dream.

The dreams can rock someone's world. The therapist's world, the dreamer's world. The whole world is out of alignment. To do this work with others does not mean to teach, preach, know. To do this work with another person is to sit with him and commiserate around the one truth that is going to lead him to another truth and from there another truth and another truth. This is the moment to have with a client.

If the therapist preaches, the client is not going to be in the moment with the therapist. The client is just going to be defensive. The work of the therapist is to understand what something means for the dreamer. Unraveling this is moving into the very essence, the core, of the dreamer's consciousness. Each dream is incredibly personal, has a great deal of meaning and is also wrapped up with memories.

This is the spirit of the dream. The dream cracks into the essence of the soul, into those feelings that are so precious we do not want to share them if we know them. If we do not know them, then we get very sick.

The dream is like a map to the that core, to our essence. It takes a long time, there are many corridors and there is a great deal that would confuse the journey. The therapist's job is to get underneath needing to know what is what in a dream in order to find what the client knows in the moment. It is about finding the only truth that the client can know in a precise moment.

Most people cannot stand in any kind of truth and say, "I am that I am because I feel this." When we cannot do this, we are actually then infecting each other. Without the dream, the world is an insane place.

One of the most seductive things that we can do when working with dreams is to take a position because then the position becomes our intention. When we take a position, we have a vested interest. We are no longer advocating for the dream, for the dreamer, for God. We advocate for our position – especially when we are personally invested and feel we cannot afford to be wrong. The position of a therapist should be positionless.

The work is about finding the truth, and the truth is variable. What we know in one minute about a dream can be different the next minute. It is all part of the ever-changing, emotional, spiritual reality that we carry inside and which can confuse us. When we get confused as a therapist about where a client is on the map of his journey, we just wait until the next dream and the confusion is cleared.

Often, I leave a session more confused than when I began and I feel I cannot wait for the next dream to clarify my confusion. But I have to wait. If we try to figure it out because we feel uncomfortable not knowing, we jump out of the discomfort and jump away from where we need to be because we can never figure it out. It is not about figuring it out. Even if we figure it out correctly, it does not matter.

For, the work is about helping a person open to this psychotic world and to feel into that world and to learn from that world. It is not about making accusations or summations, for every summation, every accusation, every confrontation leads to more uncertainty and the next unknown place. There is no definitive smoking gun; there is only the unfoldment of pain, trauma and God's love.

Stage Four

The Art of Feeling

We take for granted the whole idea of feeling, but it is an art in and of itself. We have the art of prayer and the art of meditation, the art of love – what about the art of feeling?

A big part of this work is to not assume that we know how to feel. Rather, we need help in understanding that we probably do not feel.

An actual feeling is a feeling as it arises in a dream. The work from the dream – the homework – is to go back and feel the feeling.

Generally, the consequences of feeling are great. Real feeling sets the psychological reality of the ego reeling, and as a result, we often react. We do not do our homework assignment because our big NO comes up. Part of the reason for this is that we become confused about what is happening to us. It is as if we have taken a drug – as if we are going psychotic in some way.

But there is another part of this, which is that we do not know what to believe when we feel. Feeling in this way, the way the dreams show us, simply changes our reality. Sometimes we do not want our reality changed.

This is part of this work. It does not matter if the feelings are difficult or painful or trauma-based, for many are. It does not matter if the feelings are filled with love and energy. We still jump away, we still have a reaction, we still project our feelings out and make them about someone else.

We even project the good stuff, wanting to fall in love with someone so we do not have to feel all the love inside of us, just for us. Or, we want to hate someone or believe someone hates us so we do not have to feel our own self-hate. It is far "easier" to feel feelings through something in the world than to feel them through our own inner experience.

As long as we do not own our feelings, we cannot heal. As long as the feelings are projected into the world, they are not ours and the Divine cannot help us.

Self-expression is not necessarily feeling; it is often the reverse. When we express ourselves, we are living two realities – what we express and what we feel. These two things are often different.

When we do not feel our feelings first and own them as ours, we never really let their acid do what it needs to do. The feelings get blurted into the world. This causes a reaction from the world and then it becomes all about our struggle about our feelings – assuming they are even feelings – or our own struggle with ourselves against others, which is a complete distraction from our own personal journey.

This is why the dream reality and the world reality are often sharply distinct or separate in the initial stages of this work. For the way we act in the world based upon who we believe we are is very different from what our dream reality requires us to do as we open up to our feelings.

At some point, everything comes back to the same moment. What we have accomplished of accepting our own transformation can then be put into the world. But when we make the world the vehicle for our changes rather than our own work or spiritual journey as shown by the dreams, it can become very confusing.

If we go inside, find our true selves and then emerge, we can be in the world doing what we feel is right for us – our work or community work or being in our families. When we have ourselves and our connection with the Divine, we can enter into the world without projection.

When there is an extraordinary flowering of the human spirit taking place in relationship with the Divine, it can be in the world. This is possible when each of us takes responsibility for our own connection, our own love and our own negativity. Every time something arises, in this kind of community, we can bring it back to our own work, our own process. Even if another person was "wrong." When a group or a community has this kind of process, the result is an incredible way of being together.

This is the secret sauce, this is the miracle. This is an opening to the security and the safety of people who are grounding their inner lives and their caring for one another through something inside of themselves. People can let go in that environment and not because everybody "makes nice." We can all feel and respond in this kind of environment because we all have the capability to relate to this deeper love, too.

Finding the love is not just about falling in love with someone, although we all want a flesh and blood person, too, not just a spiritual beloved. Ironically, when we get the love on the inside, we can also get it on the outside.

If we have the love on the outside and not on the inside, however, even if the relationship is good, we will either lose it or not live it to its fullest.

There is a flip side to this as well. When we have the love on the inside, we can be tricked into believing we do not need anything at all in the outside world. We may say, "Oh, I am okay with just me and my dog, thank you very much." This can be as much of an avoidance as when we look for love on the outside.

We can have both – but the love on the inside must come first.

That Which Is Yours Will Always Return

When we are afraid of losing something, we are really afraid because we have already lost it. What we try to keep hold of is usually something that is not ours to keep. Holding on is just compensation for the fact that we have already lost who we are. When we are not living who we are, we hold on to the things that are not who we are and then we lose them anyway because they are not ours to begin with.

What belongs to us inherently wants to stay with us, wants to keep coming back to us. It can take on many different forms, but we often do not recognize that it is us, that it is coming to us for us, because we lost it through trauma or we gave them up because we felt we could not keep it. So, anytime anything good happens, anything that relates to the self we lost or to what belongs to us, we end up pushing it away.

When we lose ourselves, we look for something to replace it, something that is not ours in the first place, striving to hold on because it is not really ours. We do this while all the time avoiding what really is us, what would give us all the fulfillment and would be ours.

When we give up what is not ours, what we have

taken as a replacement for who we really are, this is Dying to Self, stepping into the cross, stepping into the Alchemy of transformation. This is becoming the child again and coming back to who we are.

It is almost as if we become the Christ because we become the one who has to stand in the cross, who has to die to self in order to become reconnected to who we really are, to the soul self that is immortal. When Christ died on the cross, he did not die so we would not have to – He was showing us how to do it, how to die to self.

The Excruciating State of Beingness

To live in a state of being is excruciating. It is not really scary or painful, for fear and pain are really ways that simply open us to our beingness. When we face into the child self, when we become the child self, we feel the love and we begin to spiral into the center, into the moment.

But we quickly jump away. We all find a way to put on the brakes. We project it onto something that does not go anywhere – our music, cars, men, women, anything that will disappoint us. We want to be disappointed. We want the disappointment so we do not have to feel the unbearable lightness of being. The intensity of beingness.

Jumping away from our beingness is so automatic that we do not even know we are doing it. But when we open to the miracle, the real core where joy and primalcy can come, to the heart of the Divine, it is just excruciating.

Consciousness implies death in everything we know, in everything we do, in everything we think, in every day. It is almost as if we will blink out of the world of creation. In fact, we will not exist – not in the way that we have always existed.

Living Out the Dream

The experiences of the Divine in a dream are real, and they are meant to be lived. That means that what happens in the dream in the latter stages of the work, is meant to be lived out in the world.

In the early stages of the work, our initial experiences are with pathology so we can see how we are living the pathology through projecting it onto others. We live this dream out in the world, too, whether we know it or not. But what is different in early stage dreams is that the context is more negative or pathological than what we believe. It seems to us as if the dreams do not necessarily agree with what is taking place in our outer lives.

From this point of view, the dreams look more symbolic, more metaphorical because we do not understand what is happening. We do not understand how pathology throws all kinds of things around to make us believe something else is happening.

Pathology does this to avoid visibility. The projection of the past into the present is all part of the labyrinth of confusion, the spider's intricate web of confusion that we find ourselves in as we first begin to follow our dreams.

But as we grow to understand, we can see the truth of these dreams. We can see how pathology infects us. In seeing this, we can see how we cover the truth with things that seem okay to us, but are really not.

Then, in later stages of the work, the Archetype comes, loving us. Now instead of showing us how we live the pathology out in the world and suffer through the pathology, the dreams flip the other way. As this process unfolds, the Archetype is able to shine through. Our vision clears; we become clear. We feel the presence of the Archetype and feel that the true experience of the dream is no longer trying to show us something that we do not know and that is negative. The dreams begin to give us what was there all along – what we could not get to or what could not get to us.

The relationship with the Divine through the dream simply needs to be lived or experienced on a conscious level. In this moment in the work, it is the only thing left to do. The Animus or the Anima comes into the dreams to give us these gifts.

In the advanced stages of the work the gifts start coming and these experiences of the Archetype start happening. These miracles are not meant to be metaphorical; they are meant to be lived every minute of our lives. That is the challenge at this point in the work, to begin to know and feel every minute, all the gifts.

So, if the Animus kisses a woman in a dream, she can walk around all day long being kissed. He is not just kissing her in the dream, He is kissing her every minute. It is like an eternal kiss that does not have any past or present. It does not merely last three days or three hours; it is eternal. It is a never-ending kiss.

Living that feeling that over and over eventually becomes consummate with the experience of being alive.

This is living out the dream. This is the beginning of enlightenment. To be enlightened means to receive the light, to receive the love, to receive the relationship. Not just as a feeling, but as a relationship that has characteristics that are reflected in the dream. We can live the dream in the conscious world. He comes to us in a dream in the way He means to be with us in that moment – and He will come again in a different way in the next dream.

Epilogue

The Gift of the Three Rocks

Dream:
I am in a basement with the Animus. I feel covered in a warm, thick sensual glow, almost like honey. He shows me a huge box of red, glowing rocks. Many are wrapped up in some kind of silk fabric.

The rocks were magical, alien, different, red hot, not of this world – but they were not burning the silk. It was a miracle they were not burning the silk – like the burning bush that did not devour the bush.

He told me many things.

"You worry about traumas from the past, past lives. Traumas from times of persecution. There are many throughout time. The real issue is that it all started at 0 AD, during the time of Christ."

"People who were persecuted since the time of Christ also lived in the time of Christ. It all started there. Those people have come back to take positions they had then."

He showed me how I had hidden my rocks. He said. "You still don't know who you really are."

He said, "Many people are afraid. The psychological traumas cover the spiritual trauma of persecution, which goes back much further than the memory of persecution, for they may have been persecuted many times. It all began at 0 AD This is when a gift was given many people."

The holy blood, the holy grail, is not just the holy blood of Mary. Not just the offspring of Jesus and Mary.

The holy blood is the gift that was given. It is the three rocks.

Those who received the gift of the three rocks were condemned and persecuted for the knowledge of the three rocks. But the three rocks are more than just knowledge. It is not just knowledge of the mind. The three rocks have power.

The ones who have been given the gifts have grown to hide them. The reason the earth is in a crisis is because those who have been given gifts have lost the will to stand in those gifts. We would have to believe in ourselves in a way we do not like to believe in ourselves because of the memory of the persecution.

For me, it was hard to accept how glorious, how powerful, how potentially earth-changing this gift could be. The individual capability to make such a difference. It somehow bordered on the idea of being a megalomaniac if I believed it.

But in the dream, he showed me how I have hid my rocks, despite the fact that I have done so much. I felt terrified when He told me that I still do not know who I am because I do not know why I do not want to know.

I do not want to know who I have been in the past and I believe many people feel this way. We do not want to something deeper about ourselves – maybe it was something we were persecuted for or maybe it would change our understanding of ourselves in an incredibly radical way.

The greatest gifts. I am beginning to realize that Christ was not the messiah, although he was a great teacher. He was given three rocks, too. They were all given three rocks – Paul, Peter, Thomas, Mary, all of them. Those given the rocks had the same potential, the same learning, the same capability as Christ.

All of that was projected, dumped, onto Christ. For everyone with the gift could be enlightened. In Catholicism, they call it sainthood. Anyone with the three rocks can be a saint in this way.

What does this mean? It means standing in God's love. That is it. It is that simple.

All of this was put on Christ. He had doubts, like we all do. He had his moment on the cross when he cried out in anger to God. But he turned it around. Everyone else handled the persecution poorly or differently. Christ did not which is why he was the better teacher.

The question is – Who are we really? We are all potentially capable of doing what Christ was doing. We are all capable of having that kind of impact on the world. But, the difficult part is that no one wants to be the one, when we could all be the one.

All humans on the planet could be the one.

But we would rather single out one person and make him be the one. The Archetypal Realm exists for all of us and is there to help us. But the idea that Christ obtained the connection with God was wrong. We can all obtain the connection with God.

This is why people have been persecuted, like the Cathars. They all attempted to do as Christ taught – to follow him, to be him. This is the big divide.

In psychological terminology, if we believe we are Christ, we are considered immediately insane. But what if the idea of being Christ, of being Mary, of being any of them, is really not a big deal. Not if we stand in the evolution that has been offered to many people, if not, ultimately, everyone.

I have been terrified of this message. The gift, the three rocks, are still here.

In the process of working with dreams, when you are given this gift, the dreams come to support that gift. If there is a fourth stage in this work, this is it. It is the realization of being able to achieve the goal of living with the power of the three rocks. This creates the evolution of the species. The evolution of us all.

Dreams Like Pearls

From Christa Lancaster

'The Truth must dazzle gradually, or all the world be blind."
~Emily Dickinson

Dreams like pearls:
In the catacombs of light and love with the Man
In the sarcophagus as a pupa in a chrysalis
Blinding light, love and healing

I.
Two nights ago:
I dream I am climbing up a hill with a woman who is carrying a tiny baby. At the top of the hill, a woman comments on the baby, asking a foolish question. We carry on inside the a large house in which many people are busy with healing and dreams. Marc is meeting with a small group including Deb and others about a project. There is a feeling of excitement in the air, a sense of engaged energy, like bees in a bee hive. All of a sudden, I am surrounded by a brilliant light. I can't see anything else but the light. I feel blinded and it scares me. I scramble to find my sun glasses. I can't find them anywhere. I stop. I stop looking. I stop running from this light. I stop struggling. I surrender.

Through the blinding light I find myself in a different plane of consciousness. Marc and I are working with R, a very brainy guy who did this work years ago. The session feels more like a hands on healing. He and I surround R, along with his wife, C, with a field of love. We enclose him with our bodies.

Before our eyes he shrinks and becomes a tiny baby, complete with tiny baby glasses, miniature versions of the glasses that R the actual man really wears! We fold around him in love.

II.

I write my dream down. Step one. I need to write the dream.

Then, I remember my dream this morning in which I visit Annie in her bed at a retreat which seems like my old boarding school, Wycombe Abbey. She has a pretty pink blanket with some holes in it. She is sad; tears roll down her cheeks. I want more than anything to climb into bed with her and cry. Instead I leave. I end up in a long corridor with some darkish liquid snaking its way out of the kitchen down the hall. I am torn between looking after the problem and finding my way back to Annie.

It is Sunday morning. I start to cry. Marc comes back from his early walk with the dogs to the tower. I lay my head on his chest and quietly weep.

I have not felt the tears I need to release. I cannot move ahead until I have let myself soften into my tears.

The tears come and I soften. When I am soft I can feel love. When I am soft I can let in love.

III.

When you have been drenched in love, you know what love is. My dreams come to remind me of what I knew.

In the first dream I am pierced by light which is love, Divine love, God's love, his love, her love... extraordinary love. This is the love and light down in the tunnels of the catacombs. This is the consciousness of love.

This is what I was scared of. I was scared of the love. I remember it. When I follow the Man into the tunnels I am actually returning to what I knew, sometime, somewhere. Real love. A field of consciousness both dazzling and blinding. I had the tunnel dream. It was the beginning of an initiation into a new level of consciousness. I merge with the sticky pupa of the chrysalis. I am changing. I wrestle with the goat in me who wants to be in charge, worry and stay aloof. She does not want to die in me. I struggle between haughty goat control and liquid chrysalis love girl wanting to emerge. Another layer of pathology loses ground. Soft, strong girl in me surfaces. Tears melt goat; grief dissolves old, protective walls.

Why do I fear the love? What happened to me in another time and place that makes me want to flee this love like honey? I am seeing down the tunnel of time, the continuum, or pipe line between worlds, eras, cultures, life times. I see a clear pathway...the soul, my soul knows neither time nor space... the soul moves along the pathway, backwards and forwards...

What if it is true that Mary herself was the grail, the vessel, for the blood of their union? What if Mary was an enlightened woman who shared a vision with an enlightened man who together agreed to step into an historical time and place to bring an embodied, sensual form to a pole of consciousness we might call the Christos, the light, the love into a dark, distorted world of corruption and lies?

What if the tunnels of light and love bend back in time from now to then?

What if we all are vessels?

What if the light and love is the Christos available to every woman or man willing to look at every aspect of their darkness to become vessels for this consciousness?

What will we find in France?

Why am I so reluctant to make the commitment to the little house we have found to rent?

What if what we fear most is the pole of love that is eternal?

What do I really fear?

How much love can I bear?

IV.

In one week, Marc dreams about three molten rocks, the spiritual gifts we are given while I dream about the blinding light of ineffable love. In my dream we come together, physically close with a third person, a woman, wound around each other to heal the man of the mind and watch him return to the baby of his true beingness. In the dream we are warm touch and sensual embrace; the body is the way the light can move through.

In the sensuality of the dream the healing is no longer even about the dream. As the humans we are, we become the vessel for the love, the carriers of the light. The dreams bring us into the sensual experience of love: warm, human, holding, skin to skin, flesh to flesh, breath to breath, heart to heart, with a white star bursting in the center of our bodies, one heart, one love, one molten rock burst into flames.

Glossary of Terms

Alchemy - The transmutation of the basic material of feelings into deep, inner spiritual change.

Anima - The Archetype who embodies the feminine principle. Her role is to support and nurture the dreamer in preparation for a relationship with the Animus. Part of this role is as a healer through acceptance of the true self.

Animus - The Archetype who embodies the male principle. His role is to empower the dreamer through relationship and to bring the lie of the ego self into awareness. For women, the relationship is as a lover and a teacher; men usually work with the Father to begin with, for the Animus is also a son of the Father. Once a man has become the Prodigal Son, he comes into a younger brother relationship with the Animus.

Archetypal Realm - The unconscious realm of the psyche where the Archetypes live and where the dreamer is in the soul self and thus can be in relationship with the Archetypes.

Archetypes - Beings in dreams and in the psyche whose role is to bring the dreamer into relationship with the Divine. Archetypes are vessels of love and essence.

Big Lie - The beliefs held by individuals about their particular lives and by society as a whole that keep the individual from the journey to the soul self and relationship with the Divine.

blood tears - In the myth of Persephone, the seeds of the pomegranate that bind Persephone to the underworld forever; a motif for the love the dreamer has been missing.

child self - See *soul self.*

conjunctio - A Jungian term meaning "to come together"; the essence of Divine relationship which requires that the vessel of the individuated soul be separate from the Divine at the same time it is of the Divine.

dark mother - A dark feminine aspect of pathology that can manifest in many ways including the devouring mother, the shaming mother, the needy mother, etc.

demon - See *pathology.*

Dying to Self - The process of letting the persona/false self, which is created in compensation for the separation from the Divine, die in order to become the true self, the self that is in relationship with the Divine and knows the love of the Divine.

ego - A field of consciousness that has the capability to contain consciousness from both the subconscious and the world.

essence - An individual's particular capacity to feel God's love in a direct and personal way. A person in essence has the heart that can know God and can experience God's love through the feeling realm; one of the rungs of Jacob's ladder. Jacob's Ladder also includes sensuality and grace.

grace - The direct encounter with God and the highest octave of receptivity of the Divine; one of the rungs of Jacob's Ladder. Jacob's Ladder also includes essence and sensuality.

gyroscopy - The ego's attempt to continually balance itself by keeping the dreamer oriented in the outer world where the warring factions of pride and shame, worth and unworthiness, reign supreme. See also *puer*; *senex.*

Jacob's Ladder - A motif for understanding the elements of receptivity of the Divine. The rungs of Jacob's Ladder are essence, sensuality and grace. To be entirely receptive to the Divine, the dreamer must have all three receptors open.

pathology - A force within the psyche whose intention is to keep the person from feelings that would open him or her to the Archetypal Realm.

polymorphous perverse - The period of development in early childhood when the child is freely amoral and has no self- consciousness. The child is open to his or her immediate sensual exploration and all the feelings associated with it.

primalcy ("primal sea") - The deeper levels of vulnerability, such as pain, yearning, need, passion that represent the flow of energy from the realm of personal need and expression.

Prodigal Son - For male clients, after having rebelled and gotten lost in the Big Lie, it is the return home to the Father as the boy, with all the feelings of inadequacy – in the adequacy – with the Father. Upon his return, the Prodigal Son understands his problem, feels the core pain and is gladly reinstated with the Father, who joyfully welcomes him.

projection - The justification of why people feel the way they feel by believing that their fear and pain are the result of something external - others, the world and life situations. When projecting, an individual is avoiding true feelings that would ultimately lead to the Divine.

psyche - The vessel that holds the imagination, soul, dreams, feelings and even the pathology of a person; the container for the dreamwork journey; an inner room where the theater of transformation can take place.

Persephone - For female clients, the embodiment of the descent into the Archetypal underworld, a Dying to Self, to become the beloved of the Animus, leaving behind the shadow of the dark mother.

second death - Dying to the Divine; coming into direct relationship with the Divine; experiencing congruency between the self and the Divine.

sensuality - The ability to feel God's love in the body in a way that is unique to each person; the capacity to sense the power, passion and intensity of being in relationship to God through the tactile self; one of the rungs of Jacob's Ladder. Jacob's Ladder also includes essence and grace.

soul self - The true self capable of relationship with the Divine; often manifests in dreams as a child.

trauma - Occurs when a person becomes disassociated from the soul self and feelings through the repression of fear; the point at which the person stops being the child; the place in the psyche where the child self waits to be reclaimed. Trauma is not a traumatic event but the repression of feelings that can happen as a result of a traumatic event. It is possible to have experienced traumatic events without having trauma in the psyche.

triangulation - The appearance in dreams of three elements: the dreamer, the Archetype, and a feeling or being (often a child) through which the dreamer can come into relationship with the Archetype; precedes Alchemy.

Valkyrie - The manifestation of Divine connection and relationship in women; the capacity to be entered and received and empowered by her relationship with the Animus; the Valkyrie wields the sword of discernment and leads others to the Divine.

wound - The place in the psyche where the original hurt or trauma that caused the separation from the Divine resides.

§